HOW TO LAUNCH A
SUCCESSFUL SERIES

HOW TO LAUNCH A SUCCESSFUL SERIES

Your Book Launch Survival Guide

HELEN B. SCHEUERER

Contents

A note on spelling

Australian/British spelling has been used throughout this book, unless material has been directly quoted.

Introduction

"I feel like I'm on the precipice of really levelling up with my career."
(Author Diaries, August 19th, 2021)

All authors dream of making a splash with their launches; of getting those much-sought-after bestseller tags on Amazon, of making a renowned list, of selling thousands of copies – they dream of *success*. However, as much as it pains me to say this, writing an incredible series is not enough, though many of us wish it was. There are so many moving parts to a successful author career: writing, marketing, publishing and everything in between. How we approach our launches is a massive aspect of this.

As of writing this book, I have launched three successful fantasy series, and one of the many things I have learned is that each launch is different. There are endless options, countless strategies, various experiments to play with, and a world of opportunity out there when it comes to how you can make your series a success. The book you're holding in your hands explores all of these facets, alongside mistakes made and lessons learned from yours truly, as well as other successful authors. It's my hope that this candid look at launches provides you with the tools you need to craft and implement the launch of your own series.

Personal story

I launched my first series in 2017 with my debut fantasy novel, *Heart of Mist*. It was the first book in my bestselling trilogy, *The Oremere Chronicles*, and it paved the way for the success of that series – and, if I'm honest, my entire career. *Heart of Mist* launched live on August 31st, priced at $0.99, and quickly gained its orange bestseller tags in numerous categories, on various Amazon stores around the world. I would go on to use the blueprint of this launch for the rest of the series and then tweak it for what came next.

I've spoken about this previously, so I won't go into too much detail, but… I did not anticipate the level of success that came with this series, nor the fact that from then on, authors would ask me how to market their books and how to launch their careers in a similar fashion.

Since then, over the last six plus years, my launches have changed drastically. I started off with live $0.99 launches, then moved on to short pre-order campaigns and, eventually, to longer full-priced pre-order campaigns. The exact strategy often depends on which book in the series I'm launching.

Nowadays, I use a combination of hard and soft launches (thanks to Elana Johnson for the terminology) and a range of price pulsing strategies, depending on where I'm at with a series and what book is being released.

Defining "successful"

One of the things I love about the *Wish I'd Known Then* podcast with Sara Rosett and Jami Albright is the question they ask all their guests: "How do you define success?". The beauty (and difficulty) of this question is that the answer is different for everyone and always will be.

Rachel McLean, award-winning and bestselling author of the Dorset Crime novels and the Zoe Finch detective series, defines her measure of success as "at least 50% of people reading book one read through to the end (normally book six). Also if pre-orders are constant or rising throughout the series."

Bestselling fantasy romance author Carissa Broadbent defines success in terms of "stickiness" and enthusiasm: "If a launch isn't a bestseller, that's totally fine. What I want from my series is for them to steadily grow in readership and continue gaining new readers who absolutely LOVE it."

Author Meg Jolly, who writes the bestselling D.I. Daniel Ward crime thrillers as well as *USA Today* bestselling fantasy fiction under the name Meg Cowley, categorises her definitions of success in two ways: "From a reader point of view – if it's rated 4.5 stars or above, if readers are excited about it, engaging with me personally (on socials/via email) to rave about it, if they reread it (the highest honour, in my opinion!), and if they talk with other readers about it to recommend it... plus if they demand more books or spin-offs because they want to stay in the world with those characters. That's success for me!"

She went on to expand upon "success" from a business point of view: "If readership (pre-orders/sales/etc.) grows with every book, and they are consistently rated 4.5 stars or above (that level of quality matters to me, it also means I'm targeting the right readers), I know that's a healthy series."

My own definitions of success are also along these lines. I like to see steady growth in pre-orders, a steady stream of highly rated reviews coming in, and – perhaps a more intangible thing, but important nonetheless – readers engaging with the book on various platforms.

For the purpose of this book, we need a "universal" definition of success, just so we stay on the same page. In my mind, a successful series meets the following criteria:

- It earns out what the author invested in it (for me upfront production costs have varied up to $5,000 AUD per book, in addition to ongoing expenses like advertising/marketing/newsletter promo)
- It's highly rated in reviews
- It continues to sell steadily, long after the release of book one
- The pre-orders of subsequent books outdo the previous books
- It contributes to a steadily growing income for the author

All my series do this.

Before we go any further, I encourage you to deliberate on your own definition of success, and to be realistic. You might want to consider:

- Upfront costs/financial investment
- Royalty expectations based on similar books/series you've written

Your definition of success might be completely different to my own and the authors' above, and that's okay, but I do want you to keep it in mind as you read through the rest of this book.

Why this book?

I love reading nonfiction books about craft and publishing, and in 2022, I published my own nonfiction debut, *How To Write A Successful Series*. Since then, I've received many questions about marketing and launching books – essentially, what comes *after* the book or the series is written. Thus, *How To Launch A Successful Series* felt like the natural next step.

When I originally started writing nonfiction, the broader topic that fascinated me the most was the idea of the "long game" when it comes to writing and publishing careers, and I believe that successfully launching multiple series is a big part of that. So, I've combined my personal experiences with the lessons I've learned from other authors thriving in our field to provide you with an ultimate guide to your options and potential strategies for launching your book series.

In these pages, you'll find insights from bestselling authors like Rachel McLean, Meg Jolly, Carissa Broadbent, Steffanie Holmes, Krystal Shannan and many more.

Who this book is for

This book is for the author who has written or is writing a high-quality series and is looking for advice on how to approach launching said series in the most effective, strategic way for long-term success.

It's also for those people who read and implemented the guidance in *How To Write A Successful Series* and are looking for advice with the next steps.

It can also be applicable to authors who may want to breathe new life into an older or existing series.

If you're looking for a survival guide to launching your series, this is it.

What this book is (and isn't)

This book will cover an array of book launch strategies. It will lay out your various options and help you decide what will work for you, depending on your individual goals.

Throughout this book, I'll be as transparent as possible as I explore my own launch experiences, and will endeavour to save you the hassle of making the mistakes that I've already made. It's my hope that this book acts as a menu from which you can pick and choose what will work for you depending on your chosen genre, the way you work and the platforms you favour.

However, this book *won't* tell you how to *write* a successful series – it will assume you've already written one. If you haven't written your series yet, consider returning to my previous book, *How To Write A Successful Series*. I'm not usually one to toot my own horn, but it does contain some rather vital information on market research and understanding series as a form that you might very well need in order to launch a successful series. As we'll cover briefly, a lot of the more powerful strategies require an author to have baked elements of marketing into their fiction prior to launch.

This book starts off with the basics of understanding launches and delves into the initial groundwork of a series, because the work that leads to a successful launch starts long before publication day. Stick with me – it'll be worth it.

This book *won't* teach you how to build a platform, though I strongly suggest having at least one channel to launch to (a website, a mailing list, a social media page, etc.). Finally, this book won't teach you how to master paid advertising. That's not my forte and there are many other, better books dedicated to that topic.

How to use this book

This book is about launching books, specifically books in a series. I have no doubt that some of the lessons within will be applicable to standalone titles as well; however, the majority of what you're about to read has been written through the lens of launching a series. I'm of the belief that every launch of a new book in a series is the opportunity to relaunch the previous books, so keep that in mind too.

You'll notice an underlying theme throughout this book: working out what suits you. Advice flies around left, right and centre in this industry, but you don't have to listen to it all. What works for one author may not work for you, or perhaps only part of their method may work for you. That's more than fine – in fact, I encourage you to pick and choose the advice you take and the strategies you implement, as long as they suit you and as long as the goal is to prioritise launching a successful series.

If you're anything like me, you might be tempted to skip ahead and read through the sections that are most relevant to you and where you're at in your career. However, I recommend that you read cover-to-cover first and then revisit the sections that resonated with you the most. Although I've done my best to split topics into neat chapters and subsections, the truth is that a lot of this information is interlinked and a lot of the strategies we're about to explore work best with one another, so the information will serve you best when digested in the overall context of the book.

So, shall we begin?

Section I: Groundwork and Pre-Launch Strategies

ONE

Book and Series Launches 101

"For the first five or six years, I was still learning what I wanted to write and how I wanted to write it."
—Krystal Shannan

BEFORE I STARTED PUBLISHING in 2017, my idea of a book launch was a fancy in-person event at a bookstore (with plenty of wine) where the author would sign books, mingle with readers and celebrate their achievement of writing and publishing a book.

I've done a launch event like that on several occasions, but especially when it comes to indie publishing, there's a lot more to launching than milling around a shop and making an awkward speech with a glass of cheap bubbles in your hand.

So, let's get the obvious question out of the way: *what is a book launch?* I know, I know, the basics can be boring, but you'd also be surprised at how many people aren't quite sure what a launch entails.

A book launch can refer to two things:

1. The actual date your book releases to the world
2. The promotional period either side of that date

A launch is all about the planned marketing and distribution strategies an author (or publisher) organises in order to boost the sales of an upcoming or newly released book. It's arguably the most important (or at least the most well-known) stage of the entire marketing process. The strategies I'm referring to can include anything from traditional media coverage, social media and advertising to paid newsletter promotions and hosting an in-person party or signing.

In my experience, book launches can range from huge 100+ person events at bars, bookstores and private venues, to a quiet launch of simply hitting "Publish" and emailing your newsletter list. These options, and every launch style in between, have their place when it comes to releasing a series, but what I'll endeavour to do over the course of the book is lay out the various options and help you decide what's best for you and your titles. Before we get into the nitty-gritty details, let's take a look at those different types of launches…

Big traditional launch

This is the type of launch many of us dreamed of when we were first starting out as authors. A traditional publisher. A huge advance. A book tour with lots of signings. A marketing campaign with swag (promotional material like stickers, bookmarks and character art) and special edition ARCs (Advance Reader/Review Copies) for influencers... The thing is, this type of launch is rare even if you *are* traditionally published. The bulk of publishers' marketing efforts go towards their big-name authors, while the midlist and debut authors are largely left to their own devices in terms of marketing.

Indie launches - soft, medium and hard

In my experience, as well as my extensive research, indie authors tend to categorise their launches based on degrees of intensity, or a certain style – Elana Johnson refers to hers as "soft, medium and hard", while Mark Dawson refers to them as "the Beyonce, the Bell and the Dawson" in his Self Publishing Formula short course "Improve Your Launches". Over the years, I've found myself with a similar approach, particularly as I've increased the number of books I'm producing. Personally, I just can't manage four huge book launches each year.

Steffanie Holmes, who launches anywhere between six to eight books a year, is in a similar boat: "Because I launch so many books a year, I can't do a big, enormous thing every time... Half the time my brain is already on the next book while the launch is happening. I tend to focus a lot of effort on the first book in the series and the last book in the series."

She went on to tell me that there were other deciding factors – for example, if a series was doing really well, regardless of where the current launch fell in the series, she'd put in the extra effort.

A softer launch might entail emailing your newsletter list when the book goes live. A medium launch might build upon this strategy with posts to social media, newsletter swaps and some paid advertising. A hard launch might involve all of these things on a larger scale, as well as a broader outreach marketing campaign, a larger budget for paid advertising and perhaps an aggressive pricing strategy for the initial book/s in the series. As with many things in publishing, it depends on the individual author.

What we'll explore in this book are the tools to create any one of these launches, personalised to you, your goals and your capabilities. Take what you need from the options and craft your own ideal launch for your series.

Rapid releasing

This is technically a publishing strategy, but many indie authors use rapid releasing as a launch strategy as well. This is where books in a series are released in quick succession, capitalising on the Amazon New Release algorithms as well as reader excitement. If you're able to produce and publish quickly, this is a fantastic way to build a backlist and gain traction for your author career. However, I should note: as I'm not one of these authors, while this book explores the option, rapid releasing is not the focus.

Relaunching a series

Whether you unpublish a series and republish with new covers and revamped blurbs, or you simply create new editions and/or package the books in a boxed set or omnibus, relaunching a series is also a type of book launch that many authors utilise to breathe new life into their sales funnel and find new readers for a stale or stagnant series.

Kickstarter/crowdfunding

Since Brandon Sanderson's record-breaking Kickstarter (for four secret books in his Cosmere universe), using a crowdfunding campaign to launch a publishing project has grown significantly in popularity. Authors are using platforms like Kickstarter not only to fund, but to build excitement and reach a whole new audience with their launches. Backers are able to support creators they love, while also enjoying all sorts of bonus merchandise and early access to content.

Special editions/book boxes

A special edition or exclusive book box launch is usually in addition to the regular launch of a book or series. However, these have the added benefit of all the physical edition bells and whistles: foiling, sprayed edges, custom artwork, beautiful dust jackets and hardcover case designs.

They're usually accompanied by merchandise: candles, mugs, bookmarks and art prints, to name a few examples. The beauty of launches that include special editions or book boxes is that they reach a different type of reader entirely – collectors and people who love showing off their beautiful books. These people are often also social media influencers. Creating additional products like these for a launch is now part of many authors' strategies for tapping into the TikTok platform, increasing their chance of potentially going viral.

In-person events

In my experience, in-person events are becoming less significant when it comes to launches, but they still have their place, usually in conjunction with a variety of other strategies. The scope of these types of events can vary wildly: they can be huge affairs with hundreds of people, intimate signings at a local bookstore, or a stall hired at a local fair or convention. More on in-person events later!

———

There you have a brief overview of the types of book launches. Your own launches will depend on a variety of factors, and in the following chapters we'll go into everything you need to implement these strategies for your series.

TWO

How I Plan My Series Launches

"The grind of this job feels like it's getting harder and harder and demanding more and more of me for the same or lesser results than before. But I listened to an author talk the other day who basically hit the nail on the head – as hard as it gets, I still wouldn't want to do anything else."
(Author Diaries, April 5th, 2022)

I'LL BE DOING a deep dive into each of my series launches later on, as well as sharing experiences from other authors. However, before we get into the nitty-gritty, I wanted to give you a glimpse behind the curtain and share exactly what I do when the launch of a new series is on the horizon and nothing has yet been put in place.

If you've read my nonfiction before or heard me speak on a podcast, you probably know I'm a big planner. This sort of thing gives me energy and I enjoy sitting down with my calendars and mapping things out. I know not everyone is like this, and I strongly encourage you to approach your own launches in a way that energises you and brings you joy. However, I'm asked so often about how I do things that I wanted to share it here.

Before I put pen to paper with any launch plans for my series, I study the market. And I'm not just talking about bestselling comp books' content, but what they're doing in terms of their launches. I look at completed series by successful authors, as well as what they're working on currently and how exactly they're structuring *their* launches. Are they rapid releasing? (I already know that's not for me.) Are they publishing wide or in Kindle Unlimited? What are their pre-order periods like? Are they using incentives? Where are they talking about their books the most? I do all this research not to copy straight from these authors, but to assess my options according to what works for me and what works in a broader sense. There's a crossover somewhere in there, and that's where I start to dig deeper.

While I'm doing all this deep diving into the market, I also take the time to examine my own production rate and schedule. Since I'm a big planner, I need to be able to roughly predict how fast I can write and release books in order to determine my approach to each of the launches within a series. I'm able to do this because I've tracked my word counts and hours spent on each manuscript for a few years now, and I have a good idea of how long the other stages of book production take me.

From there, I work out how many books I can write in the coming year, how far ahead I can be in writing the series and how I can stagger the launches of the subsequent books. I try to take into consideration personal holidays/annual leave, potential sick leave/mental health needs, batched marketing and admin days (as I can't do more than one thing at a time, apparently), as well as turnaround time for editors, proofers and designers.

Obviously, this process isn't perfect. It doesn't overly account for when life goes super sideways, but it's enough of a plan that I feel comfortable taking a bird's-eye view of my calendar and scoping out the best possible dates for my launches in the series.

It's around this time that I start to think about the *type* of launch I'll be aiming for with each of the books in the series. We've already discussed the various types, and whether they're based on intensity or a particular goal, but for me, it really depends on the actual book in the series, as well as how long I expect that series to be.

For the most part, I launch my series starters fairly hard and I always have the next book up for pre-order – both to capture any hot interest at the end of book one, but also to let readers know that I won't be leaving them hanging and that the next book isn't far off. I like to hold their hand a little, let them know that they can trust that it won't be ten years until the next instalment. This also means that for my own comfort levels, I need to have the pre-order book at least drafted.

So, usually it's a big push for book one, followed by a less intense launch for the following book, but with a mind to put the first book on sale or schedule another sort of promotion for it, depending on how long it's been since the initial release. This is to capture a new audience and breathe new life back into the starting point of the sales funnel.

In an interview over email, Rachel McLean told me something similar about her own series launch strategy: "I focus less on launching and more on promoting book one in my series and getting new readers to start at the beginning." Author Meg Jolly offered similar insights: "I hard launch book one for maximum impact. If it's a new pen name, I invest a lot upfront, before the series launches, to build a readership who is ready and waiting for the first book to drop so that it can be successful in engaging and building its own readership right out of the gate that's excited about the series and also making sure it's financially viable to continue. With subsequent books, I do much lower key launches, really focusing on those current readers who love the series already and want more, as the pre-orders for each book snowball."

The same goes for me. The launches for the middle books in a series are generally less intense, with another big push for the finale. It's worked well for me so far, and that's the approach I have when it comes to mapping out the launch of a new series from scratch.

In my conversation with Steffanie Holmes, she spoke about how she has a core list of things to do for every launch and then a range of additional options that she picks and chooses from, depending on the launch itself. This is a similar method to me as well; there are things I'll do for every launch (which you'll see in my launch case studies), and then depending on where I'm at in the series, things I'll only do for certain books (like price pulsing and discounts).

My launches now are a more refined version of the way I've always done them, even from my very first series starter, *Heart of Mist*. It's largely a matter of understanding your own processes, restrictions and personality type.

Personally, I need to plan. Without a plan, I'm agitated and unpleasant to be around. I find it hard to focus on the tasks I need to execute if I haven't got a roadmap to follow. I also know that I'm not great at juggling too many things at once, or launching books back-to-back. I know the rough turnaround times for all the services and freelancers I use, and that makes things much easier when it comes to pencilling in the dates for launches. I know that when book two is with the copyeditor, I need to be drafting book three, and so on.

Armed with all that information, I stand in front of my wall planner that spans the entire year and, using sticky tabs, I plot out the production of each book, as well as where I think the launches will sit best. I avoid any major holidays or sales periods where I can. I also take into consideration any life stuff I've got going on at the time – for example, will I need to move house this year? If so, when's the lease up? When will I be running around to view rental apartments and potentially packing up my life yet again? Am I going overseas in the coming year? Is it possible to work while on "holiday"?

I swear, half the battle with launch planning is knowing yourself, and avoiding, as best as you can, periods of time that are already naturally stressful for you. Of course, you can't always do this, but the rough plan helps to make things simpler.

Once I've decided on the date for book one, I do it all

again with book two, book three, book four, etc. I consider where these books are in the pipeline of production and when, realistically, they'll be publication-ready. As I mentioned, I need to have the next book drafted before it's up for pre-order at the very least, otherwise that's a stress recipe waiting to happen for me.

I like to make sure my books are spaced out evenly throughout the year (ideally it would be one per quarter, but I'm still working on that), and I make sure that they're relatively consistent in the length of time between releases. The last thing I want is to set readers up for disappointment – part of launching a series is also managing readers' expectations. I'm also conscious of burning myself out with releases too close together.

When I've mapped out what I think is feasible, I add a few weeks onto that, just to be safe. I can take advantage of a longer pre-order – setting the date beyond what I think I'll need, and then having the option to bring it forward if I want to. I did this for my series finale for *Curse of the Cyren Queen* and it had the added benefit of pleasing fans who thought they were going to have to wait until November – they got it in September.

Something Meg Jolly explored in our Q&A for this book really resonated with me. She mentioned intuition and experience in the industry, and this is something that a lot of newer authors forget: it took us years to learn this stuff! And years more to learn to adapt when we need to (something I'm still working on). Meg said: "I often launch instinctively, based on years of experience. I might not have it written down, but I know what I'm doing. This is one area I can improve on – I think I could get an even better ROI (Return on Investment) if I honed the promotion and marketing aspect of this career. Even with the experience and success I've had, I think you can never know it all, and also need to be aware of your own shortcomings... This is one of mine!"

If all of this is a lot to digest, don't worry – I'll be diving into specifics in my series launch case studies later on. But for now, you might want to ask yourself the following questions:

- How long does it take me to draft a manuscript?
- How long does the editing process take me?
- How long does it take to get beta reader feedback?
- How long does it take to incorporate this feedback?
- How far in advance do I need to book my editor?
- What is my editor's turnaround time?
- How far in advance do I need to book my cover?
- What is my designer's turnaround time?
- How long does it take to proofread the manuscript?
- Do I need to book a proofreader in advance?

Other considerations:

- How long does it take for print files to be approved?
- How long does it take for print proofs to arrive and be reviewed? (This will vary in different countries and regions)
- Am I hoping to use promotional services? How far in advance do these need to be booked? (Some are a minimum of two months in advance, for example)
- Is there enough of a window to create content for launches?

These are the sorts of questions I sit down and mull over as I start to map out the overall launch plan of a series. You don't need all the answers right away, but they're certainly things to consider as you put the pieces on the board.

THREE

Know Your Publishing Options

"I have a lot more understanding of marketing and readership, so I am more intentional now... I have specific metrics I want to see for every book, which changes depending on which book in the series it is, and between series also. Knowing what I want each book/series to achieve is very helpful in achieving the bigger picture."
—Meg Jolly/Meg Cowley

WHEN IT COMES to indie publishing in general, it's vital that you know your options for how you can get your books out into the world. I'm talking about everything from the rate at which you release books, to whether you go exclusive with Amazon or wide, to whether or not you utilise pre-orders and whether or not you sell direct. Many authors use a combination of different strategies unique to themselves and their situation, and I encourage you to do the same.

In this chapter, I'm going to cover a range of publishing options that you'll need to consider before launching your series, as well as a handful of common questions I receive. Let's get started.

Amazon exclusive (Kindle Unlimited)

Ultimately this question is: where should I publish my book? It's one of the first decisions an indie author has to make when determining their upcoming launch plans.

For those who are new to the industry, publishing "exclusively" refers to Amazon's Kindle Direct Publishing (KDP) Select program, or Kindle Unlimited (KU), as it's called on the consumer's end. This service is where readers pay a monthly subscription fee and can read as many books enrolled in that service as they like. Authors are paid for pages read rather than units sold, and they're not allowed to sell their ebooks on any other retailer. For each 90-day period that the author keeps their book enrolled in KU, they have the option to run price promotions called Kindle Countdown Deals (KCDs). KCDs are limited time discounts for Kindle ebooks in the US and UK Amazon stores. The benefit of these deals is that the consumer can see the original price, the discounted price and a countdown timer as to when the deal will be over. During this promotional period, the author also maintains the higher royalty rate, even at the discounted price.

Wide publishing

Selling "wide" simply means that you publish your books across all online stores (iBooks, Nook, Kobo, Google Play, Amazon, etc.). The main benefit of this method is that an author isn't putting all their eggs in one basket regarding their income and audience. Going wide also gives you more options regarding discoverability – while Amazon holds the market share in the US and UK, there are plenty of other retailers that dominate in other countries.

Selling direct

Selling "direct" is where the author sells their books directly from their own website. This is becoming more and more popular as authors seek to create more sustainable business models that they're in control of. Selling direct can be in conjunction with selling wide (and even with being exclusive, if we're referring to print books alone), so it's not always a matter of choosing one option, but working out a combination that suits you and your business model.

What do I do?

My experience so far has been largely with KU. As you'll discover in my launch case study for *The Oremere Chronicles*, I launched the first book in the series, *Heart of Mist*, just to Amazon (but not in KU). I didn't go wide then as it just seemed like too big of a learning curve, and there wasn't nearly as much information on the different platforms and aggregators as there is now. Three months after the release, I enrolled *Heart of Mist* in KU and since then, all of my fiction titles have been enrolled in the exclusive program since their release dates (and later, since I set up their pre-orders).

I only claim to have dipped my toes into the wide method, with the publication of this nonfiction series. It is part of a long-term strategy for diversifying my income. However, I also dabbled in selling direct for my paperbacks and hardcovers. I did this for a few years via my WordPress website shop and a plugin called WooCommerce, which many authors are still using today. However, back then I wasn't aware of services and platforms like BookVault and Shopify, nor was there the same volume of advice and information regarding selling direct as there is now. There also weren't services that offered to set up your shop and systems for you.

From 2017 to 2019, I ordered and stocked books in advance at my home, and when I received an order, I signed the book, printed the shipping details and the invoice, packaged the book and took it to the post office. As I got busier, and later when I moved to New Zealand, this was just no longer possible, so I shut my online store with the intention of reopening it once I had a more streamlined option.

Selling direct is definitely on my radar now, especially with the plethora of information in the form of books and podcasts all going into detail about how to make this approach work for you and your business. *The Creative Penn Podcast* has multiple episodes on the topic (check the Resources section of this book), and Morgana S. Best's *Stop*

Making Others Rich: How Authors Can Make Bank By Selling Direct is a great place to start if this method is something you're considering.

How to decide which method is best for your series launch

You're going to see another ongoing theme throughout this book, which is: market research. The market research you do for your series will help inform you of reader expectations not only for the content of your books, but the publication of them as well. For example, when I was doing market research for my series *The Legends of Thezmarr*, I noted that the majority of the bestselling books and series in the fantasy romance/romantic fantasy genre were in Kindle Unlimited. While I was already leaning towards this strategy because my entire back catalogue was in KU, this research helped me make an informed decision about the series.

If you're unsure about how to publish your series, I encourage you to go back to your market research and the bestselling series in your genre. Consider the following...

- Where are these books being published?
- Are they wide or in KU? Is the author selling direct?

You can take this research a step further by looking into the types of editions and formats that are available:

- Ebook, paperback, hardcover, large print, special editions, audio?
- What are the most common formats and do you have the capability and funds to do something similar?

Please keep in mind that the decisions you make now are not unchangeable. That's part of the beauty of indie publishing: you have the freedom to change your mind later down the line.

A few caveats:

- You can be exclusive with your ebooks, but wide with your print distribution
- You can also sell print directly from your website while publishing your ebooks in KU
- Some authors launch wide first, giving everyone the opportunity to buy from their preferred retailer, before taking the book off the other platforms to launch exclusively with Amazon. Alternatively, some go the other way, as it can be easier to upload a title to multiple stores after a period than to remove it
- The beauty of being indie is that you can trial and test a variety of publishing methods to determine what works best for you and your readers, which is what many successful authors do

- Some authors will have part of their catalogue in KU and part of it published wide. I publish my fiction exclusively with Amazon, but my nonfiction is available on all retailers
- If the thought of publishing to multiple platforms overwhelms you, you also have the option of using an aggregator like Draft2Digital

To pre-order or not to pre-order

As you'll see in my launch case studies later, I've tried both: setting pre-orders and launching "live" (hitting the "Publish" button when you mean for the book to become available).

A pre-order period can be as short as you like, or on Amazon, up to a year in advance. In general, the arguments for and against pre-orders revolve around "rank or bank", which we'll cover shortly.

As my business has grown over the years, I've become partial to the pre-order camp, and in the chapter "Pre-Orders As A Marketing Strategy", I'll explain this in more detail. But essentially, my thinking is that if I'm doing all this marketing in the lead-up to release and have no pre-order available, readers might forget to check when it's live, and I've missed out on a sale. However, a pre-order means that while I create buzz about the series, I have the ability to convert that interest into a sale immediately. But that's just me and where I'm at in my career. Everyone's different, and this chapter is all about options, so I want to lay out the pros and cons of pre-orders for you.

. . .

The pros:

- Receiving the link to the product page in advance so you can schedule promotion and direct readers to the actual "Buy" feature throughout your launch period
- Capturing a hot lead from a previous book and converting it into an instant sale –this works particularly well when releasing in series
- Gauging the interest in your book from the pre-order figures and tweaking your budget and release promotion accordingly
- Capitalising on anticipation and giving those who might be early adopters the chance to support you
- Knowing the date of your release (without a pre-order, the general line after hitting "Publish" is that your book will be available within 72 hours of submitting it)
- Giving you a solid deadline to work towards

The cons:

- Diluting your sales rank. On Amazon specifically, pre-orders are recorded the day of purchase, as opposed to on release day – so any pre-orders an author receives on this platform

won't count towards their ranking on publication day, which waters down the chances of hitting a bestseller list
- If you're in KU, many of your readers won't pre-order; they'll wait until the book is live so that they can use their subscription to read it for free
- If you're a new author, or the book is the first in a brand-new series, some readers might be inclined to wait until the title is out before they consider purchasing it
- For some authors, the pressure of a hard deadline can be debilitating

What about timing? How often should you release?

This question comes up time and time again whenever authors are talking about launching and publishing strategies... And the answer isn't an easy one: there's no right way, only the right way for you. Only you can know your abilities and your limits.

I'm often asked about stockpiling and rapid releasing. This is where you write a bunch of books, hold onto them until you're either done with the series or a few books ahead, then release them in quick succession. This could be once a month or every two weeks. "Rapid releasing" is another slippery term, because, as Elana Johnson says in several of her author talks, rapid releasing is really just what's rapid *for you*.

I've been asked about the best practices for rapid releasing, and as someone who doesn't rapid release, this isn't really in my wheelhouse. However, Elana Johnson has a great book called *Writing and Releasing Rapidly*, which I highly recommend. Even if, like me, you're not planning to rapid release, it's a great resource for streamlining your writing and publishing processes.

A concern for a lot of authors is: once you publish the first book in your series, how do you maintain a particular publishing rate and schedule? Alternatively, once you've published what you've stockpiled, how do you maintain a regular pace? What that boils down to is tracking your data, which we'll talk more about in the next chapter. But essentially, being realistic about your capabilities, both in the way you write (e.g. how fast, how long you need for revisions) and in external lifestyle factors (e.g. if you work a day job, have kids, are a carer, etc.) will help you determine what's possible.

When I first started, I released one book a year. There were a few reasons for this:

- Originally, I had a day job
- The learning curve for indie publishing was immense and I wanted a solid foundation of knowledge before I pushed a book out into the world
- With a background in traditional publishing, I didn't consider that I could write and publish more until much later
- With the big launches I was doing, I wasn't sure I could manage more than one a year

- I was still learning and refining my own writing processes – I wrote much more slowly back then
- The income was so good that I took it for granted and didn't question what might happen after the first series was finished

Since 2017, I've quadrupled my production rate, which sounds a tad insane. However, this was done over a long period of time. Here's what my publication schedule looked like:

- 2017: *Heart of Mist*
- 2018: *Reign of Mist*
- 2019: *War of Mist*
- 2020: *Dawn of Mist* (prequel collection) and omnibus of *The Oremere Chronicles*
- 2021: *A Lair of Bones* and *With Dagger and Song*
- 2022: *The Fabric of Chaos, How To Write A Successful Series* and *To Wield a Crown*
- 2023: *Blood & Steel, Slaying the Shadow Prince, Vows & Ruins* and *How To Launch A Successful Series*

As you can see, it's taken me six years to increase my production and publishing rate. Six years of learning, of trial and error and refining what works for me specifically.

Again, we'll get to that in the chapter on streamlining your processes.

However, I want to point out a few things: this clearly didn't happen overnight. It's been a slow and steady increase over a long period of time. After *Heart of Mist* I was able to write full time, which naturally helped things along. I learned about my processes at a much faster rate once I had the freedom to set my schedule to the hours that suited me and wasn't coming home mentally drained from a boring day job.

I also want to highlight that the years where I published two books didn't necessarily outdo the income of the years where I only published one book. It has been a massive learning curve for me, determining which release styles and production schedules suit me and my personality. And while I can't say for certain just yet, I may have reached my limit with four books a year.

The way I write and release has changed over time. For example, with *The Oremere Chronicles*, I wrote each book and released it when it was done. I found that as the series gained momentum and as writing became my full-time job, I wanted to be a little further ahead in the production schedule... So, in 2020 (the year I didn't publish a full-length novel), I spent my time writing as much of my next series as I could.

When *A Lair of Bones* launched in July 2021, I had already written the draft for *With Dagger and Song* (book two) and sent it to the editor, as well as outlined *The Fabric of Chaos* (book three). I was ahead with the covers and general production of the series for the first time in my career, and it felt good. It meant that I could plan promotions in advance, and on a craft level, I could weave threads back into the first few books where needed, to make the impact of the later books really pack a punch. This was my version of stockpiling. I was never sitting on an entire completed series, but I was ahead of my publishing schedule and being strategic about how and when I released the subsequent books in the series.

However, doing this or stockpiling on a larger scale does have its risks. For example, what if you've written and paid for the production of five books in a series, but the first book flops? You don't have any data informing your decisions about the later releases. A seasoned author might be confident doing this, but for most of us, it's a scary prospect. One that I considered as I moved forward with the publication of *Curse of the Cyren Queen*, as you can see in this entry from my journal: "I sat in my office before, trying to iron out a more solid release/marketing plan for the *Curse* books... If I can get my act together, I'd like to try releasing six months apart. Although it feels insanely risky to sit on a completed book while my income suffers... But it's a risk that could pay off enormously with then being able to release more quickly..." (Author Diaries, October 31st, 2020)

At the time of writing this book, I still like to be ahead in the production schedule, with a little room to breathe and pivot if something unexpected comes along. This approach suits me and my personality of being a planner and very future-driven, but everyone is different in that respect.

———

Another question I received was about "training readers": if we're supposed to train our readers on how often to expect a new book, would a larger gap between books be better in order to lessen the chance of burnout?

I'd like to address this question in two parts. First: I'm *always* in favour of lessening the chance of burnout. If the release strategy you've mapped out already strikes the chord of burnout fear in you, then I would say yes: create a longer gap between books, give yourself that buffer time and space. In the long run, no good will come from you trying to hammer out books if you're going to fall apart midway through and be unable to produce.

The second part I'd like to address is this concept of "training our readers", because I myself have definitely used this phrase somewhere along the way. In general, I've always liked the idea of managing readers' expectations in terms of release schedules; I think creating this line of communication with our audience is important. But that's just it – it's a line of communication. Once you get to know your own writing and publishing processes in more detail, it'll be easier to predict when you'll have the next book in your series out – but until that time, whether it's via social media or your newsletter, the most important thing in my mind is being honest with your readers and keeping them informed about where you're at with the process.

When I was releasing the books in *The Oremere Chronicles*, I would tell my readers "a year from now" for the next release, because I knew I could produce a book in that amount of time. With the *Curse of the Cyren Queen* books, I knew a span of six months between releases was realistic. And the same goes for *The Legends of Thezmarr*. But I only know this because I monitored my own progress, and all along, I communicated with my readers whenever I had updates to share. It's not so much about "training" your readers as it is about not leaving them in the dark.

———

I know that was a lot to take in, and these decisions are not ones that should be made on a whim. Take some time, do your research, and consider your own writing style as well as what you've got going on in your life outside of publishing.

FOUR

Streamline Your Productivity and Processes

"Must remember that I'm not a fucking writing machine. I strive for consistency and have daily word goals, but the fact is not all days are created equal. Yesterday I had a 6K day, whereas today it's nearly 1pm and I'm only on 2,500 words. Those words have been hard."
(Author Diaries, January 7th, 2023)

I'M one of those writers who loves *having written*, but for whom the act of writing itself can often be akin to pulling teeth. From the initial brainstorming sessions and hours of outlining, to "fast drafting" the manuscript itself and seemingly endless structural edits, the sheer amount of labour that goes into a book is intense.

Most of us start writing out of love: for the craft, for the genre, for the thrill… And that never quite goes away. However, something does happen when you put a barcode on your art, when you shift your creativity to a business –

which is exactly what you're doing when you're writing a series. The pressure starts to pile up: pressure to produce more, to produce better, to produce faster.

I started to experience this as *The Oremere Chronicles* wrapped up and I looked to the future. All around me, indie authors were producing multiple books a year, and I had only written and published one every 12 months. I also found that the more books I had out, the less time I had for actual writing. My time was taken up by emails (usually from readers asking when the next instalment was due out), outreach marketing campaigns, content marketing, advertising, social media... All of which served to maintain the status of the current books, but none of which saw to the growth of my series and overall catalogue.

I realised that I needed a shift in mindset as well as in my production methods. I needed to prioritise producing words; producing books in series over all else, as this is the core of my actual job. I couldn't be an author if I didn't actually write more books. So, I started tracking my word counts and I kept "author diaries" to keep track of my progress.

One of the biggest "aha" moments of my career so far was planning my production schedule for 2023 during the final weeks of 2022. For the first time, I had data on how long it took me to write and edit a book; solid, consistent data from several manuscripts to help me make informed decisions about what I would be capable of in the coming year. An author friend and I took turns helping each other iron out our plans for the year – how many books we *wanted* to write, how many we could *actually* write, how many we wanted to publish and in what order/during what months, etc.

I can't tell you the high I felt at sorting this out. And yes, part of it's because I'm a planner, but it's also because being an indie author is a business, and businesses need to be able to predict income and what sort of output they're capable of.

As I mentioned earlier, it took years to get to this point, so I'm not sitting here expecting you to run to your calendars and plot out a five-year plan any time soon. What I do want to stress, however, is that if you're serious about being a career author, it might be time to put some strategies and tactics into place that will enable you to streamline your processes and predict your output in future.

In his book *The Ultimate Guide to Book Marketing: The 80/20 System for Selling More Books*, Nicholas Erik talks about indie publishing as a "probabilities game", and how by "improving your skills in the core three areas – productivity, craft, and marketing – you can significantly raise the probability that each book you release will be successful." I took this message to heart when I read it. I had always tried to improve my craft and was always trying new things when it came to marketing, but one thing I was slightly late to the party on was improving my productivity. So let's take a closer look…

Production

Streamlining my production processes has played a significant role in the success of my series. When my processes are predictable and efficient, I'm able to better plan the books in my series as well as their subsequent launches. Getting to this stage required a lot of tracking and monitoring as I wrote, so if you don't track your word count, this is your sign to start.

Over the last few years, I've learned how the production of a book looks from my perspective:

- Creative input (reading, watching TV, going for walks, conversations with friends, market research): Ongoing around other projects
- Outlining: Two weeks
- Drafting: Four weeks
- Structural editing: Two weeks
- Beta reader feedback rework: Two weeks

Then the book is off to the copyeditor and is largely out of my hands for a month before I get it back to make in-line changes. Then it's off to the proofers. All in all, it's on my desk with me for roughly 10 weeks.

You may also find that as you work your way through your series and develop as an author, you'll need less involved help. Perhaps you'll be able to cut out the developmental edit, and only use beta readers for one round of feedback. I've certainly found this to be true. For each manuscript in my first series, I did a structural edit myself and then two rounds of feedback with beta readers. This was incredibly time-consuming and often disheartening. However, as I progressed through my career and moved onto writing my second series, I realised I had learned a lot of lessons from that first time around... So much so that I only needed one round of revisions with my more recent books. It shaved almost two months off the production process for each book in the series.

Over the years, I have streamlined this and experimented with which writing methods work best for me. For the majority of my career, I had been attempting to write in sprints – a common approach for many writers. I'd set a timer, write, and then when it went off, I'd get up and make a tea, stretch my legs, etc. I managed well enough – I was getting my books written and meeting my deadlines. However, a call with a coach shed light on something that changed my whole outlook on how I write.

After four years of being a full-time author, it was pointed out to me that I'm an incredibly focused person. I hate interruptions, I hate when my concentration is broken, and I love to shut out the world and block out all the noise. And my then way of writing clashed with that. Every time I was about to sink into the manuscript, the timer would go off and I'd be taken out of my focus tunnel.

The coach I was speaking to gave me permission not to sprint. She told me I could sit in my chair as long as I wanted, getting my words down. She even encouraged me to set up a tea station in my office so I didn't have to leave the room to make my cuppa. (Not great for the physical health, I know, but that's a topic for another day.)

Prior to this rather simple revelation, it took me months to write a book, even as a full-time author. After this one phone call, I finished a 101,000-word draft in 22 working days. I've drafted all my books this way ever since, and it's how I came up with the turnaround times for my production schedule.

My point here is not that you should write a book as fast as you can, or never leave your desk. It's that I experimented with my methods, I found a way to do things that suited me and my personality better, and then I made it part of my streamlined production process.

I know now that when I'm writing a book, I can't do much else. I need to ignore marketing and admin for the most part and hunker down to get that first draft done. And sure, sometimes this is easier said than done, but I'm much more easily able to identify why and where I'm struggling, and how to fix the situation where possible.

Sadly, I can't tell you how to be your most productive self. I can't tell you that you'll work better in the morning than in the afternoon or evening. I can't tell you that if you have a coffee at 7am, you'll have a mental crash by 11am. Only you can learn these things about yourself, and they'll be different for everyone. The only way to learn is through trial and error, and by tracking what works and doesn't work for you.

Start a journal, a spreadsheet, or whatever tickles your fancy, and every time you sit down to write, note the time of day, how long you wrote for and how much you wrote. You can also note down particular circumstances, like the weather, whether or not you were interrupted, if you put your phone on aeroplane mode or not... Jot down anything you think might have impacted or influenced the way you worked.

My notes for this purpose can range from things like

"Depressed, distracted" to "Very fractured, stressful sleep last night. Already anxious that my focus is going to be shot to shit" and "Interruptions: messages/notifications and roadworks".

Over an extended period of time, you'll start to see patterns emerge. It might take you months, or even a year to work out these details and their inevitable variables. But don't despair – you'll learn them eventually, and once you do, you'll know how to wield this knowledge to your advantage.

I've learned that not only do I do my best creative work in the mornings (drafting, reworking manuscripts), it has the added mental benefit of giving me a sense of achievement that fuels me throughout the rest of the day. I have also learned that in order to feel that sense of achievement for the day, I have to prioritise production. For me, this means working on projects that will become actual books first thing in the morning. Whether this is drafting or editing, I need to be working on a manuscript each day in order to feel some sense of progress before I can move onto tasks that feel more like maintenance – like social media or managing my inbox.

All of these lessons, while seemingly small, have contributed to my overall work strategy and schedule, and thus, my overall productivity. It's taken me years to refine this process, and there are still times where I slip up and venture into emails first thing in the morning, or start replying to Instagram messages. If you're anything like me, you might need to learn the lessons several times before they stick.

The takeaway here is to put in the time to learn about

yourself and how you work best. Once you have, you can optimise this knowledge to increase your productivity across the creation and launch of your series.

———

The more books you have out, the more balls there are to juggle in terms of production. Sure, there's the writing and editing, but while that's going on, you're also liaising with cover designers, formatting books, researching and everything in between. You need to be able to make the most of those pockets of time when one manuscript is out of your hands to make headway on another, and this is exactly what I did and continue to do when mapping out my production schedule.

Marketing

Over the course of your career and throughout your market research, you'll notice content and marketing techniques that work well in your chosen genre. Make note of these, try them yourself and assess whether or not this method worked for you. Very similar to the trial-and-error nature of writing itself, finding the marketing approach that works for you is vital for the success of your future launches.

Marketing is a constant learning curve that should be monitored and optimised for the long term. Throughout this book, I'll be talking about batching and repurposing content for your book launches, because I'm all about making life easier, particularly around launches. We'll delve more into content marketing in its own chapter, but again, the key here is to iterate and tweak and save anything that works to reuse at a later time.

For example, I know that with every launch there are particular types of social media posts or newsletter content that always do well, without fail. Those are things like title reveals, cover reveals, unboxing videos and pictures of me with the book I'm releasing. Every piece of content like this is used with every launch. Sometimes I'll even use the same caption as the content I've posted before, just with an updated photo.

The same goes for my newsletter – I like routine and schedules, so I created a rough plan for my newsletter. It goes out twice a month (more frequently around launch) and in the lead-up to a launch, I repurpose content and templates that I've used before, always tweaking it according to the current release but using the general structure that has proven itself in the past. More on that in the chapter on newsletter marketing!

Admin

Another element of launching and your career in general that you'll want to eventually streamline is your admin. The more books you release, the more of those pesky admin tasks you'll have to stay on top of.

Not all that long ago, I realised there were too many moving parts to my business plans and strategies. I had a spreadsheet for social media, lists and spreadsheets for my launch tasks, and another spreadsheet entirely for my newsletters. I needed to rein things in so I could see everything that was on my plate from a bird's-eye view.

Several suggestions were thrown at me as to which platform/tool/service I could use to bring it all together. In the end, however, one of the simplest solutions worked best for me: Google Calendar.

I mentioned this as a tool in *How To Write A Successful Series*, and since then, I've utilised it even more, adding more calendars that I can hide and show as I see fit, depending on the tasks I'm currently working on. I now have individual calendars for:

- Personal
- Admin
- Book Production
- Client Calls
- Finance
- Launches
- Newsletter
- Outreach & ARCs
- Paid Marketing
- Patreon
- Social Media
- Street Team
- TikTok

As I mention in the section on launch marketing, I've learned that I work best in batches, so every quarter, I try to set aside an entire week dedicated to marketing and admin tasks.

Reflect and reassess

One thing I come back to after every launch is this quote from Chris Fox's *Launch to Market: Easy Marketing For Authors*: "Every novel you write is another brick in your self-publishing fortress. Each time you place one, do it deliberately. Use the lessons you learned from previous launches to make this one better. Then make the one after that better."

I always make time to question if/how/why something is working or isn't working, and if it will work again in future. I ask myself whether I can optimise a strategy or tactic, or whether a particular tool or service was a waste of money.

I encourage you to block out some time after each release to figure out what worked and what didn't, and to actually write this down somewhere!

Once you've figured out what works for you and what you can/can't achieve, make sure you continue to refine your processes, your strategies and your goals as you progress through your career. If there's one thing that's certain in this creative life and this industry, it's that *change is constant*. With each book you write and publish, you will change and develop as a writer, you will learn new things, and things will change around you. You need to be able to implement these lessons to continue to grow as an author and as a businessperson.

The most successful authors in this industry are the

ones who are never done with learning, be it about the craft of writing itself, publishing or marketing. Keeping yourself educated is one of the most important lessons you should take away from this book. As a career author, you should always be striving for improvement and finding new ways to better yourself and your process.

FIVE

The Cost of Launching a Series

"I have to try my best not to worry about money. That was all on a constant loop in my head last night and I couldn't stop it…"
(Author Diaries, August 25th, 2021)

LIKE MANY PEOPLE, my relationship with money has always been complicated, and as someone who really struggles with numbers, I find it hard to wrap my head around the cost of publishing and launching at times. The tricky thing for me is that it's never quite as simple as paying an upfront cost to produce and publish a book. Cover designers, editors, proofers, printing fees, paid newsletter promos, etc. all come out of your bank account at different times – and then there are the services that charge monthly, plus annual fees like email providers and book reporting software. Often I'm working on the production of a few books at once, so it can be hard to keep things organised when it comes to the money going into them.

I'm getting overwhelmed just typing all that out. So first, let me state the obvious: I'm *definitely not* a financial expert, and the content in this chapter should not be interpreted as financial advice.

Now that's out of the way, let me start at the beginning of what I've learned so far about the cost of launching a series...

When it came to *The Oremere Chronicles*, I didn't have a budget. Not in the sense that I had unlimited money (that certainly wasn't the case), but in the sense that I didn't sit down and add up the funds I had at my disposal and what I was willing to spend. All I knew was that I wanted the very best of everything, and I wanted there to be little to no discernible factors between my books and those that were traditionally published. My cover designer was an award-winning designer who freelanced for the Big Five at the time, my editor was phenomenal with over 20 years' experience in the industry and some of my favourite fantasy books to her name, and the rest of the people on my team had similar credentials. I spent about $5,000 (AUD) on each book in that series, which at the time of writing is about $3,300 USD or £2,600, for context.

When I released *Heart of Mist*, I had a job supporting me, and I had savings that weren't earmarked for anything in particular. I also wasn't paying off a mortgage, nor was I financially supporting anyone other than myself. I know not everyone is in such a fortunate position, but that was the situation for me at the time. By the time I was preparing to launch the sequel, *Reign of Mist*, *Heart of Mist* had earned out its expenses, and was earning enough not only to support me on a full-time basis, but in addition, to cover the cost of the next launch.

However, I was only publishing one book a year. It wasn't until I started preparing to release the *Curse of the Cyren Queen* series on a faster schedule that I realised just how much expenses added up when you were paying them multiple times a year, and how scary it was when the success of the series wasn't yet determined.

I don't regret the money I spent on those earlier books, because every time I worked with my amazing editor, I learned something new. The whole experience made me a better writer in the long run, and it also gave me the skills to create cleaner drafts and recognise the quality of editors in the future. Those lessons were invaluable in the broader sense of my career.

However, I've come to learn that the longer you're in this job, the more you can streamline costs and the more you'll want to, especially if you're releasing multiple books a year. The costs of launching a series can add up, and you want to make sure that you're getting the best bang for your buck.

There are plenty of ways authors can condense their costs: perhaps you won't always need a developmental editor before your copyedit; perhaps an ARC team will step in as eager proofers in lieu of a professional proofreader; perhaps you can get a discount if you buy your covers in bulk, or book multiple promotions at once.

In recent years, I've assessed and tweaked the costs of my series plenty of times. For example, I have now changed cover designers for each of my series. This was a combination of wanting the best return on my investment and minimising costs where I could. The covers for my most recent series are actually the most affordable covers I've had to date, and they're also the most to-market. Before, I was paying upwards of $700 (USD) per cover, and now it's $250 (USD).

Similarly, for my first series I paid over $1,000 (AUD) for the creation of my fantasy map, one that had to be updated with each book in the series. For my third series, I opted for a more affordable designer, coming in at $165 (AUD) and with no need to update with each book. It's made no difference to reader reception or to my sales.

Previously I paid a professional proofreader in addition to a high-quality copyeditor. Now, I have a team of early readers who are just as hawk-eyed who read the final typeset pages before they go to print. That decision alone has saved me $900+ (AUD).

Where I've saved money, I have either put it back into the business in the form of advertising or influencer marketing, or I have kept the costs low and made the money back on the title even faster than I usually would have.

I also always try to put aside money for unforeseen costs. For example, in the last year or so, in a bid to minimise costs, I sought to trial a new editor. He was absolutely lovely and I got on with him really well. He did a sample edit and I paid him to edit a prequel novella in the lead-up to the main book. All went well until he edited the main book. To this day, I really don't understand what happened, but his attention to detail went out the window and there were mistakes left in the manuscript that I just couldn't get past. In the end, I had so little confidence in the book's polish that I knew I had to pay for an additional proofread, an expense I hadn't planned on. Luckily, because of how I organise my income and expenses, there was money in the bank for this and I could rest easy with the publication of the book, knowing that it was up to the standard I required.

———

How much it costs to launch a series is completely up to the author and how they want to spend their money. For some elements, it can be a matter of costing cash or time; for others (like covers, in my instance), some things are just out of our wheelhouse and need to be outsourced. But if you're feeling the strain on your wallet, here are a few things you can do to keep costs on the lower side:

- Swap services with other authors
- Invest in editing software so you can at least cut down on one round of editing costs
- Skip the in-person launch events
- Ask for a discount if you bulk-buy covers
- Buy pre-made covers (I've seen some impressive ones for as low as $35 USD)
- Learn a skill yourself (like formatting)

SIX

Perfecting Your Back Matter

"If a reader has gone all the way to the end of the book and is continuing to flip through the additional material, you have a real fan! The back matter is a great place to make a connection with these fans."
—Whitney Hill ("Leveraging Back Matter Content") on Writer's Digest

THIS CHAPTER IS a brief but important one, as what you do with your back matter can play a huge role in the overall success of your series. Back matter can mean the difference between an incredible sell-through rate and leaving warm readers outside in the cold.

What is back matter? Essentially, it's any content that goes in the back of your book after the end of the actual novel content. When indie authors are discussing it, back matter generally refers to the call to action (CTA) to buy the next book and the CTA to sign up to your author mailing list. Both are incredibly important.

Sign-up form or pre-order: which to put first

I've had this conversation a bunch of times with other authors. Ultimately, you need to prioritise what's most important to you at the time. Remember, you can always come back and change your back matter (outside of launches, I have a reminder in my calendar to do this every quarter where needed).

So, what's important in that moment? Is it capturing the pre-order sale while the reader is fresh on the heels of a cliffhanger and chomping at the bit to know what happens next? Or is it getting them on your mailing list so you can build up excitement for the next release more gradually? Those are the priorities I generally flip between, though some authors also add in a request for a review.

For me, if there's a pre-order available for the next book in the series, my first link is to that. If I've just finished a series and don't have a pre-order up yet for a new series starter, I spotlight my newsletter link. But in most cases, I feature the pre-order link first (because capturing the sale and income is my priority), then a link to sign up to my newsletter (with a reader magnet offer).

Again, it's completely up to you which you choose to put first, and you can definitely have both! Just know that the first link will be the higher-converting one, and the more CTAs you use at the end of the book, the less likely it is that your reader will actually take action.

Doing your own formatting

Back matter is the main reason I encourage authors to do their own formatting where possible. Particularly when you're writing in a series, you want to be able to update the back matter of each ebook with every release. For example, as you release the next book, you'll need to change the "Pre-order now" CTA to "Buy now" or something similar. Additionally, when you finish your series, you can add something like "Binge the whole series now" to showcase the fact that the series is complete and readers won't have to wait for the following books to release.

This is a task I include with every release in every series I'm publishing: ensuring that the back matter of the previous books is up to date with the correct links and the correct language.

Depending on your rate of publication and the number of books in your series, this may become an arduous task, so you could always opt for something more generic like linking to the series page itself and including something like, "Read the series here".

Formatting your back matter

For the longest time, I was resistant to the type of formatting I use now because it didn't "look right". I used to make sure there was a page break between the end of the book and the back matter, so the reader could sit with the ending for a moment. That was short-sighted of me, and I still wonder just how many pre-orders and subscribers I missed out on over the years because of it.

Now, I avoid page breaks and images and instead use an ornamental break (a scene divider) so the back matter flows right on from the end of the story. This stops readers closing the device before they've seen my message, which I keep brief.

Since I've changed the style of my back matter, I've seen a much higher conversion rate both in pre-orders of the next book in my series and in sign-ups to my newsletter.

My friend, author Sacha Black, adjusted her back matter in a similar fashion, removing even the ornamental break altogether, and saw a newsletter sign-up rate of 25%.

My back matter

I've tried numerous variations for the actual written content of my back matter over the years, and in the end, the simplest, shortest messages work best, in my experience. Here's how mine currently reads:

Want to know what happens next? Pre-order [Title], Book 2 in [Series Title] now.

* * *

Remember that deliciously steamy scene in [location]? Want to read it from [MMC]'s point of view for free? Download your spicy bonus scene here.

. . .

And that's it… Simple, right?

After that, I include a chapter break followed by a note asking for reviews and offering another reader magnet, but that's just a personal choice. The bit that packs a punch is those few lines included above.

If you combine open loops and cliffhangers (as discussed in *How To Write A Successful Series*) with simple, well-formatted back matter, your sell-through rate for your series should be solid.

SEVEN

How To Time Your Launches

"Every now and then, I'll have a split-second daydream about this launch going well, really well..."
(Author Diaries, December 16th, 2022)

ONE QUESTION I get asked frequently when it comes to launches is about timing. It's always some variation of "How should I stagger my releases?" or "How much promotion should I do in the lead-up?" or "What should I do after the release?". All are valid questions, but there's a common word throughout: *should*. This word plagues the indie author community like nothing else. It's a constant thorn in our sides, a nagging sensation at the back of our minds. *What* should *I be doing? I* should *be doing more...* And believe me, I've puzzled over every iteration of these questions as well. Even now I still catch myself going down the path of *Should I...*

The subject of how to time the launches of a series is rife with this kind of thinking. We're constantly turning to the author beside us, wondering if we're doing things "right". But I'll say it again: there is no right – only what's right *for you*. The timing of the launches in your series depends on a myriad of factors that I can't possibly account for here and now.

All the authors I spoke to during the research of this book had vastly different answers, and that's because they all work to their own schedules and personality types. Bestselling author Carissa Broadbent told me: "I don't worry too much about timing launches. They happen when the books are done. I do long pre-orders for subsequent books in a series so readers can pre-order the next book immediately, but shorter ones for book ones or standalones."

Thriller author Rachel McLean described her current strategy to me as a period of four weeks where she utilises her weekly newsletter to share the blurb, an excerpt and launch announcement, and then a reminder and thank you for reviews. She also records a face-to-camera video at the crime scene for each book and posts it to social media on launch day. Additionally, she runs Facebook ads "for the first two weeks or so after launch", and for a new series, she would implement all these strategies and a lot more, with a bigger emphasis on ads.

Clare Sager told me, "Depending on the length of the series, how the series has performed, and the length of time between releases, I'll put more or less marketing and promotional work into the release," which is something I do myself as well.

So, because we're all so different, what information can I share here to help you with figuring out the best timing for your own series launches? Well, I can provide a framework whose timing you can tweak to suit your own launch schedule.

In his book *Launch to Market: Easy Marketing For Authors*, Chris Fox talks about three general phases he usually works with: launch preparation, the launch and autopilot. My method is similar, only my framework is made up of four stages: soft promotional push, the ramp-up, launch and the catch-all. (These aren't official industry terms by any means – they're just how I look at the different phases of a launch period.) How long each phase lasts is up to you and the style of your launch strategy. For example, if you were rapid releasing, these phases might only last a matter of days, or perhaps a week each. For those of us who are releasing more slowly, they could last for weeks or even months.

In my most recent launch, here's how the phases looked for me:

- Soft promotional push: Four weeks
- The ramp-up: Four weeks
- The launch: Four weeks
- The catch-all: Four weeks

If it seems like a lot, it actually was – perhaps a little too long, in hindsight. But the thing is, it's all completely flexible, and it's more about mindset and the type of content that you're pushing than anything else. The beauty of it is that you can pivot at any time throughout the whole launch period, so if you find a particular type of content or a specific style of marketing is working better than others, you can adjust your plan accordingly.

Let's take a look at what's involved in each phase now...

The soft promotional push

This is the early stage, where you're talking about your upcoming release here and there, but not posting every day, not screaming about it from the rooftops just yet. During this phase, I do things like reveal the title, share teasers of the cover (not fully revealed), talk about the process and share where I'm at with the book (for example, I might share with my followers that I finished the manuscript, or sent it to the editor). I also do a countdown to the cover reveal, and in the background, I rally a team who will help share the cover on reveal day. I also schedule any tours needed.

Depending on where I'm at in the series, the pre-order may already be up with a temporary cover (a black-and-white, text-only image), but if it's the first in a series, I prep book one to go live on pre-order for the cover reveal date.

Things often feel a bit quiet during this stage, but think of it as a warm-up. You're slowly introducing people to the idea of your upcoming release and doing the work in the background to prepare for when things really kick off.

The ramp-up

This is where I start to go hard on building the anticipation and hype around the launch. It's during this phase that I reveal the cover and start sharing the pre-order link to the book. This is to my most important platforms: my newsletter and my social media profiles. Hopefully all the buzz about the cover reveal will lead to some pre-orders early on. Usually someone creates the book's page on Goodreads as well (you can also do this yourself), so you have another link, another platform to promote your book on. You can mix up your CTAs from "Pre-order now" to "Add to your TBR on Goodreads" – this is particularly good for people who are waiting for the book to come out in KU if you're enrolled.

On cover reveal day, I make a point to thank and repost anyone who is sharing the cover, particularly those who volunteered to share it when I did the call-out during phase one. I save all these images (using the account handle as the filename for easy crediting later) and put them in a folder for that particular book, thus creating a bank of images I can use for promotion going forward. I then schedule these images featuring the cover of the upcoming book on social media (including OG poster credit, of course), alongside titbits about the book.

This is also where I start to share teasers from the book itself: quotes, tropes, hooks – all to build that excitement in the reader for what's coming up. If it's a launch of a later book in the series, I try to strike a balance between promotion of the new release and of the first book in the series, so new readers know where to start and I potentially gain new audiences for the beginning of my sales funnel.

If I'm offering a pre-order incentive, this is also the stage where I start to heavily promote it. The featured link on all my social media profiles will direct to a list of links hosted on my website, and the pre-order usually takes top place on the list during this phase of promotion.

During this period I'll also be recruiting my street team and ARC readers. I'll check in with any tours I've booked (sometimes these need to be booked up to two months in advance) to see if they need anything else from me. If I've booked an ARC campaign with them, I'll need to make sure the ARCs are being sent out at the right time.

I'll also be doing outreach marketing while the buzz for the book is ramping up, which capitalises on any exposure I'm getting via things like the cover reveal. On several occasions now I've pitched an influencer, and because of the cover reveal, they've already seen my book and put it on their TBR, meaning they're more than happy to accept a copy for review.

All of this content (or a variation of it) is included in my regular newsletters as well, along with a longer excerpt of the upcoming book (via a BookFunnel link). This is usually the first few chapters of the book to whet my readers' appetites.

Where possible, I schedule my social media and newsletter content in advance so it's one less thing to keep track of.

The launch

This is the time immediately before, during and after your launch, depending on how long you want this phase to be. After a bunch of experimentation, this phase usually lasts two to three weeks for me – the week before launch, the launch week itself and the week after.

This is where my countdown posts go a bit bonkers and I send out a newsletter weekly. I share this content with you in the chapter on content marketing, so stay tuned for that.

If I'm trying to hit any pre-order goals, I share this too. Readers like knowing they're helping you hit milestones. Whenever I've shared a goal, readers have supported me by sharing it on social media, and I've hit that goal soon after.

At this point, I'm posting once, sometimes even twice a day. I'm sharing everyone else's content for the book as well – ARC reviews, live reader reactions, more of those cover images I saved in the previous phase... I'm always sure to thank everyone who's posting and commenting, because these are the people who are contributing to the buzz about your book – they're important!

Often during this stage I take a moment to pause and share with my readers the behind-the-scenes emotions and nerves of launch week – they like to see that you're human, after all! I find that a softer moment like this can really resonate with people.

I check that all my scheduled content is correct and ready to go live at the right times. I send my launch day newsletter with all the live links (more on this in the chapter on newsletter marketing), and I try to reply to anyone who writes back with words of congratulations.

I nudge anyone who agreed to post a review, telling them that the link is live and they're able to cross-post on various platforms now, and again, I share any five-star/outstanding reviews to social media.

The launch phase is always rife with distractions, from notifications and anxiety to trying to get other work done in and around the madness. You can get a better idea of all of this in the launch case studies towards the end of the book, as well as in the chapter on my launch snapshot.

The catch-all

This phase pretty much does what it says on the label. This is where I try to catch anyone who may have slipped through the cracks of the big launch period – the people who may have been waiting for the book to become available in KU but forgot about it, the people who missed my launch newsletter, the people who were about to click the "Buy Now" button but the baby started crying and distracted them... All of these people were warm leads and I don't want them to go to waste, so I don't take my foot off the launch promotion accelerator just yet.

I keep heavily promoting to my main platforms. I send a "mop-up" newsletter (again, more on that in the chapter on newsletter marketing). I also continue outreach marketing. While the buzz is still fresh, this is the best time for me to be seeking out new reviewers with large followings of their own. They might have seen their peers sharing the book around launch time, which primes them to say yes when I approach them offering a free copy.

During this time, people are receiving their pre-ordered print copies and sharing unboxing videos; they might have actually had time to read the book and share their thoughts. If the content is favourable, I'm sharing this like wildfire on my platforms, and thanking people like crazy for their support. Yes, it's a lot of work, but every time I've done it, it's been worth it – and you also get the added benefit of connecting to your actual readers and fans. They remember moments like this.

So, where does it end? That's completely up to you. Personally, I like to bookend the catch-all phase with an announcement for the next book in the series. This is usually already up for pre-order, so some readers will have already seen it and even pre-ordered it, but that doesn't make it any less of an occasion in my experience. Readers are over the moon to discover that the next book is already in the pipeline, and this can sometimes lead to a boost in sales of the first book for those readers who like to know where the series is heading before they commit.

At some point, I really need to focus my energy back on the next project, so I slowly wind down the massive push of a launch and dip back into a softer promotion style until the next launch is closer on the horizon.

That's not to say I don't promote at all. As you'll see in my launch case studies, the promotion is ongoing; it's just that my mindset for these launch stages shifts in order for me to progress with the next book.

When should you launch your book?

Another common question that pops up all the time is "When should I launch my book?". This can mean which season, which month, which date, which day of the week... I've received every single one of these questions at one time or another.

I believe that as long as you're not launching a first-in-series on a major holiday or during an election period, it's generally not going to make a huge difference to your success. Remember to check major holidays in your primary customer country, not just your country of residence, because often these don't match. Be mindful of how holiday periods may affect things like printing and shipping times, or how launching a full-priced book in the midst of everyone else's Black Friday deals might impact your sales... But apart from major clashes with holidays, sales periods and perhaps big traditional publishing releases in the same genre, being an indie allows you to experiment and work out what suits you best.

You may also want to be mindful of the commitments you have in your personal life – clashes with family holidays or birthdays etc. Ultimately, consult your calendar both in terms of the wider world and your personal life and make sure it's a period of time where you can be present and active on your platforms.

Finally, it's worth noting that like mine, the timing of your launches might change over time. You may find you can release more or less than the previous year, and this should always be considered when you're working out how to stagger the releases in your series.

Section II: Launch Marketing

EIGHT

Reviewers and ARC Campaigns

"I just hit 'Send' on the ARC campaign for B&S *and I actually feel sick to the stomach. There's no putting this thing back in the box now. Do I feel this terrified every time? Or does this book have a unique, torturous hold on me? I know I need to take the pressure off this launch, but knowing and doing are two separate things."*
(Author Diaries, December 16th, 2022)

IF YOU'RE OVERWHELMED by the thought of creating ARC campaigns for your series, as you can see, you're not alone. There's nothing quite like sending your freshly formatted book off into the hands of 50 strangers to stoke the flames of anxiety.

First, what's an "ARC campaign"? An ARC (Advance Reader/Review Copy) campaign is simply where an author (or publisher) sends out a number of copies of a book to reviewers ahead of a title's release. Their purpose is to garner early reviews and create buzz before a book's launch, as well as provide social proof in the form of reviews on the title's sales page.

An ARC is a copy of the author's book that is as close to publication-ready as possible. It might have the odd typo or formatting issue, but otherwise it's been edited, formatted and proofed. In other words, it's a clear representation of the quality of work and publishing that the actual book in its final form will provide.

Most of us indies send out digital ARCs, though sometimes we eat the cost of sending print copies, particularly if it's to someone with a significant platform. But for the most part, this chapter will be referring to e-ARCs.

Why do I need reviews?

I've touched on some of the reasons reviews are important above, and truth be told, it's not a subject I want to dwell on for long. Some authors can get away with no reviews on release, but I haven't met any of them. Most authors I know, myself included, go to great lengths to obtain early reviews of their book before release in order to generate excitement with readers, to provide social proof on sales pages, to use for promotion, to boost algorithms and to meet criteria for paid promotional opportunities.

I've implemented ARC campaigns for every single one of my releases and they've always contributed to the book's success. Chances are, if you're reading this book, you probably already understand the importance of reviews, so let's get into the details.

How to find reviewers

Whether you're a brand-new author or an established one preparing to launch a new series, finding reviewers can be a tricky balancing act (read: a pain in the arse). You want to make sure that you're finding the right people to review your work, people who enjoy your comp titles, so you need to be picky, but not so picky that the pool of reviewers is minuscule. However, the beauty of launching in series is that if reviewers like your first book, a decent percentage of them will be keen to read the next, so you're not starting from scratch with your ARC team with each subsequent book.

Here's how I've found my reviewers for each of my series launches over the years:

- Newsletter call-out: I email my list to see if anyone is interested in an ARC
- I create a Google Form, which is essentially an expression of interest form, and put it on my "Links" page where all my social media profiles direct
- I post call-outs on social media
- I find genre-specific ARC groups on Facebook and post call-outs there
- I reverse-engineer reviews from comp titles and approach the reviewer directly via their platform (e.g. "I saw you liked X; you might like my book…")
- I contact tour companies (more on these in the chapter on paid promotion)

What does a call-out look like?

Here's one of my most recent call-outs:

ARC Readers Wanted!

#epicromanticfantasy

ACCEPTING AMAZING REVIEW COPY REQUESTS

I'm looking for Amazon reviewers to review ARCs of my upcoming new series starter, BLOOD & STEEL. If you like:

- Enemies to lovers
- Slow-burn spice
- Found family
- Magic and monsters
- Woman in a man's world
- Training sequences
- Epic quests

…then this book is for you!

Release date: February 16th, 2023
    Genre: Epic romantic fantasy
    Heat: Scorching
    Comp titles: *The Witcher*, *The Bridge Kingdom*, *From Blood and Ash* & (an adult) *Throne of Glass*.

Note: This is an adult work, not YA like my previous books.

Blurb: [Insert blurb here]

Reviewer Requirements:

- Reviewer must be able to leave a review on Amazon (as this title is exclusive to Amazon)
- Reviewer must be willing to leave an honest review
- Reviewer will post their review to Amazon as soon as they receive the live link (February 16th)

Request Instructions:

Comment below with the following...

- Confirm that you can review on Amazon (and in which country)
- Let me know if you can meet the review deadline
- ARCs will be going out within the next few weeks, and I'm looking for readers willing to consider giving an honest review chiefly on Amazon, with fingers crossed for Goodreads, TikTok and Instagram where possible.

I've got limited review copies, so do let me know ASAP if you're keen! ARCs (mobi and epub) will be sent via a certified BookFunnel campaign.

THANK YOU SO MUCH! Can't wait to share this new series with you all.

I'll message you directly for your email if you express interest.

I have used the same basic format for every call-out with each new release and it always garners a great response, especially when accompanied by the book's cover.

I will say, however, the whole "message you directly" is now a thing of the past. Since my last release I've realised just how much work it is to directly message 50+ individuals from my personal Facebook account. Originally, I liked this method as I could see when people had seen my messages (as opposed to ending up in a spam folder), but with such big ARC campaigns now, I don't have the time to do this anymore. As of writing this book, I've converted to a Google Form setup and that final line now reads, "Please fill out the form".

The Google Form asks a series of questions (similar to those listed in the street team section below) to ensure that the applicant is the right fit for the book. When sign-ups close, I review the responses and eliminate where needed, before taking the list of email addresses and sending a bulk email to those who wish to review. This one email saves me hours and hours of time compared to my previous method. Here's what it says:

Hello there,

Thank you so much for expressing interest in receiving an e-ARC for [Title]! I'm thrilled to tell you that you've been chosen to receive a copy for review.

Shortly, you'll be receiving an email from BookFunnel with the link to download your book.

Please be sure to post your review to Amazon on release day [date].

Cross-posting your review to other platforms such as Goodreads, Instagram and TikTok is also greatly appreciated.

If you have any questions or concerns, please don't hesitate to reach out to myself or my assistant [email address here].

Thank you so much for taking a chance on this book. I truly hope you enjoy the adventure!

Happy reading,

Helen

We'll talk more about managing ARC teams shortly.

Targeting specific reviewers and a more formal pitch

You might find that you want to reach out to particular bloggers or influential reviewers in a more formal sense, which is great! This was the driving force of my ARC campaign for *Heart of Mist*, and it's something I still use today when there's someone specific I want to target for a review.

In this case, I personalise my email or message to them as much as possible. I address them by name and reference a recent, relevant review they published (ideally of one of my comp titles). It never hurts to say how much I enjoy their content either.

By this point I will have created a media kit for my

upcoming release, and I include a link to this, asking them to see if it's something they might be interested in. I make it clear that I'm happy to provide an e-ARC. (Unless I'm deliberately aiming for a print book feature, I always make sure to be specific that the ARC is digital or expenses can get out of hand, fast.)

What's in the media kit, I hear you ask? I'll cover media kits in a whole section of their own a little later on.

And just so we're clear, anyone I approach in this manner still goes into the spreadsheet. They might be someone I need to follow up with later on as well, and it's so helpful having all your reviewer outreach information in one place.

Keep records (where possible)

On that note: I keep a record of everyone who has agreed to review the current release in a spreadsheet. I have a different sheet/tab for each group/platform where I found said reviewers, and each spreadsheet includes:

- Name
- Email address
- Country (so I know which Amazon store their review will be posted on)
- ARC sent (I include the date I sent it)
- Notified book is live (checkbox)
- Follow up (this is if I need to chase them up)
- Amazon link (where I include a link to their review)

- Next book? (if they've expressed interest in the next book, so I know to reach out to them next time)

Keeping these sorts of records allows me to see at a glance how things are tracking in terms of reviews for release. It also highlights who follows through and who doesn't. If a reviewer has a track record of accepting ARCs but failing to review, I won't accept them the next time around.

Managing your ARC team

Before you start searching for reviewers, I recommend having a system or process in place for how you're going to manage your team. That way you can manage their expectations as well as your own.

There is no right way to manage an ARC team – again, you need to work out what suits you. I know authors who manage their teams via private Facebook groups, separate newsletter lists and Discord servers. Author Elle Beaumont manages her campaign in two ways: "I have a newsletter-only street team and a Facebook group I manage. The newsletter is a bit dryer of an experience whereas my reader group is more active and one-on-one."

My main advice would be to make sure that the platform you use for management is scalable. This titbit is born of my own recent frustrations, and Carissa Broadbent shared a similar experience: "Usually I open a request form ahead of release and prioritize based on response. However, my current series is so popular that I know this process is going to be a bit of a mess, and I need to revamp that."

For years, I've personally used a combination of spreadsheets, emails and private Facebook messages, and in recent times, my ARC team has become too big for so many moving parts. Not to mention that the admin tasks on my plate have grown by a truckload. I've realised that I need a proper system in place in the potential event that I outsource this particular task to my assistant in the near future.

Though I'll miss the benefits of Facebook messaging (like being able to see when a reviewer has actually seen my message), I'm opting for an email list–based system from here on out.

Delivering your ARCs

Back when I was a clueless newbie author, I sent out PDFs directly to reviewers. I know, I'm cringing as I type this. Most of you probably know that that's a sure-fire way to guarantee piracy.

Now, like many indie authors I know, I use BookFunnel. BookFunnel is a paid service for authors that specialises in the distribution of ebooks and audiobooks. Amongst its many features, it allows secure ARC delivery, offers a little more protection against piracy by watermarking your files, and provides reviewers with any tech support they need to download the book. Honestly, it's been a major headache-saver.

BookFunnel offers various options for delivery of your

ARC, but at the time of writing this, the method I use is their Certified Mail option. With this feature, you can:

- Send the ARC
- Send a reminder midway through the campaign
- Send a follow-up to let the reviewer know the book is live and ready for their review

Most of the authors I know are currently using BookFunnel for their ARC campaigns. But whichever platform or service you choose to use, just be mindful of piracy and of sending out copies into the ether. Most of us end up pirated one way or another – you just don't want to encourage it by making it easy.

ARC FAQs

E-ARCs or print ARCs?

For me, the main push of an ARC campaign is *always* ebooks. There's no cost or limit to how many I can send, there's rarely any trouble with access or delivery, and there are no time constraints – it's instant. Print ARCs, on the other hand, are pricey. The author needs to front the cost for printing and shipping the book. For my chunky epic fantasy books, this can be upwards of $35 (USD), meaning a single copy already costs more than BookFunnel's current lowest price tier.

However, there is a time and place for both print and

e-ARCs. The decision completely depends on your genre and the expectations amongst reviewers there (usually shaped by what platform they're on), and your budget (as I said, it's pricey AF). It also largely depends on how much time you have up your sleeve. Print on demand usually takes a while to process, print and ship, so if you're hoping to have physical copies to reviewers prior to launch, this needs to be organised well in advance. Exactly how long depends on where in the world you are!

Over the years I've used a combination of e-ARCs and print ARCs. The deciding factor of who gets what depends on a) the reviewer's platform and influence and b) if they're already a superfan or not.

For each new release in a series, I try to determine a budget for print ARCs and stick to it. Usually this is more generous for the first book in the series, where I'm trying to generate as much buzz and visibility as possible.

How many ARCs should I send?

I get this question a lot and there's no one-size-fits-all answer; it depends on your goals for the campaign. If you want as many reviews as possible for launch day and for the first book in a series, the more ARCs the better. It really depends on how wide you want to cast that initial net.

A common concern is that the author will send out so many ARCs that it will cannibalise their sales. I absolutely understand that fear – however, the more reviews you have during launch, the more social proof there is for people who are looking at your actual sales page.

Not helpful? Sorry about that. Essentially, the number of ARCs authors send varies wildly. For context, here are some rough figures for my releases:

- *Heart of Mist* (series starter in 2017): Approximately 100 ARCs, all digital
- *A Lair of Bones* (series starter in 2021): Approximately 50 ARCs, majority digital, maximum 10 print
- *Blood & Steel* (series starter in 2023): Approximately 150 ARCs, majority digital, approximately 35 hardcovers for influencer purposes

Why the different amounts each time? It's determined by a number of factors, but mainly a combination of intuition and assessing the demand. I have seen some authors discuss in forums that they were aiming for 1,000 ARCs... I told you it varies wildly.

How far in advance should I send ARCs?

Again, this is something that depends on the individual author and how they run their team and business, but generally four weeks seems to be a good general rule of thumb. It's not so long that reviewers download and then forget about the book, and not so short that no one gets to the book in time.

We can spend ages worrying about timing this

perfectly and still potentially get it wrong. Here's a little snippet from my journal reflecting on the *Blood & Steel* ARC campaign: "The *B&S* ARC campaign was probably an example of where I jumped the gun in that respect [sending too early]. I just wanted it out of the way so I could focus on writing but any buzz from reviewers might be premature. Fuck it, I told S that I'll just think of it as round #1 in that whole seven-touches-to-sale mentality." (Author Diaries, January 1st, 2023)

Truth be told, in the end, it didn't matter – in fact, that particular title garnered more reviews in its first six weeks than some of my older titles had had in their lifetimes.

How do you handle the negative reviews?

Ahh, the dreaded bad reviews… They're bound to happen, and they happen to the best of us. The tricky thing is that around a launch period, many of us feel like we need to be checking reviews: how many are coming in, if people who agreed to post are posting, who you need to chase up, etc. Depending on an author's process, they might check reviews to mine for promotional quotes, or for market research purposes before they finalise the next book in the series… All to say, in the early days of a book's release, it can be hard to avoid seeing reviews you would otherwise avoid. So, what do you do?

Some authors I know ask a trusted friend to look through the reviews for them. If you're disciplined enough, you can tell yourself you'll only look at the four- and five-star reviews. Never look at reviews if you're already feeling a little fragile. We all handle emotions and critical feedback differently, so what works for me might not work for you. I'm afraid it'll likely be a case of trial and error.

For me, after the first few days of a release, I vow not to go on Goodreads (it can be a nasty cesspit of negativity). I check the *number* of reviews on Amazon, but won't read anything less than a four-star – at least not in the initial launch period, where it could send me spiralling. Months after release, I might be more thick-skinned.

More often than not, if I do come across something negative or nasty, I tell one of my author friends, who inevitably gives me a pep talk. The last thing I try if I just can't get out of my own head is looking at bad reviews of my favourite books, the books that I was completely addicted to. I mentally commiserate with that author, then try to move on.

General tips for reviewers and ARC campaigns

- Specify *where* you want reviews. Being in KU, the priority for me is always Amazon, then Goodreads, BookBub and social media etc.
- Create long-lasting relationships with your reviewers – they'll stick with you through your whole series (and even career)
- Expect that not everyone will review
- Be mindful of Amazon restrictions – not everyone is eligible to review, and not everyone realises it until they go to post their review
- Also be mindful of time zones – when the book is live for you, it doesn't mean it's live for

everyone, so give people a grace period before
you chase them up

Believe me, I understand how huge a task this seems, but
for me, the juice has always been worth the squeeze. Some
of my reviewers have been with me since my very first
series starter. It's a lot of work upfront, but you can
repurpose and utilise it all again and again throughout the
subsequent releases of the books in your series.

The other thing I want to note is that ARC campaigns
are a way to discover true superfans of your work. People
who are clamouring to get an early copy, but who go on to
buy your books in every format anyway.

NINE

Street Teams

"*An individual on your street team is someone who will sell your book for you. They'll do it just because they're a big fan and admire and love your work so much that they believe in what you do and want to help out in any way they possibly can.*"
—Penny C. Sansevieri, *From Book to Bestseller: The Savvy Author's Guide to Book Promotion, Smart Branding, and Longterm Success*

FUNNILY ENOUGH, an official street team is a relatively new aspect of my launch plan at the time of writing this. For my first two series, I had a street team in the loosest sense of the term – early reviewers, people who gave me a shout-out on Instagram on launch day and cover reveal day… In fact, until a reader reminded me, I'd completely forgotten over the years that I originally had a Facebook group called the Mist Dwellers for the promotion of *The*

Oremere Chronicles. However, this was nothing like the engine I crafted for the release of the series starter for *The Legends of Thezmarr.*

But let me backtrack a moment... What *is* a street team? Originally, street teams were organised by record labels to promote musicians. They would "hit the streets" to plaster flyers all over towns, move albums to more visible parts of record stores and bombard radio stations with song requests. For authors, a street team essentially does a version of this promotion with your book.

Is this different from your ARC team? Yes. People on your ARC team can also be on your street team, as there is an element of overlap in terms of reviewing your books, but a street team does more than just review. I personally have a broader ARC team and then a more selective street team.

When it came to planning the launch of my series *The Legends of Thezmarr,* I knew something was missing. I'd booked tours, gathered my ARC team and just about everything in between. It wasn't until I'd talked to some author friends that I realised for the last five years, I'd been putting off organising a street team for myself.

You read that right: five years into being a full-time author and I had no official street team. It just goes to show we can't (and don't have to) do everything all at once. Reminder: you can pick and choose which elements to implement in your launch, and try different strategies with each new release and series.

So, about three and a half months out from the launch of my new series starter, I got serious about creating an official street team. Teams vary wildly across different genres and the authors themselves, but I knew I wanted something super interactive, where the readers involved felt special and would want to hang around for the next book, and the next.

For my street team, I decided I would do a five-week promotional push: three weeks prior to release, release week itself and one week post-launch. (In hindsight, that was too long, but we'll get to that later.) I also knew I would run a weekly challenge where each participant would go in the draw to win a prize, as well as an ongoing challenge, for which there would be another winner drawn at the end of the whole promotional period.

There are a lot of moving parts here, so just bear that structure in mind. Before I go into the details regarding challenges and so on, I want to show you how I recruit, the platform I set up and how it all comes together. Bear with me!

The recruitment form

After chatting to a bunch of author friends and researching my comp authors, I found that one of the most common ways to recruit readers for your street team was to use a Google Form.

I spent some time reading other authors' forms and picking out what I liked and didn't like, and then brainstorming other ideas that suited me, my books and my brand. From these exercises, I knew that my form had to state:

- What was expected of participants

- What I was offering, both as an experience and in terms of rewards throughout the promo period
- When the promo period was taking place and for how long
- That not everyone who applied would be accepted
- That the team would be hosted on Discord (a platform I prefer to Facebook)
- That the participants had to be over 18 to join (particularly important for me, as previously I'd written YA and *Legends* marked my shift into adult fiction)
- That if members were successful, they would be contacted via email ahead of the promotion period

All of these factors were front and centre at the top of my form. I felt it was incredibly important to manage participants' expectations from the outset.

Next, I wanted to make sure this form made it easy for me to weed out anyone who was just seeking a free book, or anyone who had dodgy intentions. As such, my form was on the more extensive side, but I wanted to be comfortable with everyone on my team. I figured that if they were invested enough to spend five to ten minutes of their time filling it out, that was probably a good indicator in itself.

So, what did my form ask? Here's the list of

questions/criteria:

- Name
- Email
- Country of residence
- *Blood & Steel* is an epic romantic fantasy novel. The content warnings are: explicit sexual content, violence, bullying, explicit language, implied threat of sexual violence and death. Are you comfortable with this content?
- Please provide your Discord username if you have one. If you don't have one, you can leave this blank. However, please know the street team exists on Discord and you will be required to create a username. Discord is a free platform
- Please check all the platforms you belong to [with a list of platforms]
- Why do you want to join Helen's street team?
- Please link to a previous review of one of Helen's books
- What was the last romantic fantasy or fantasy romance book you loved

Since that street team promotion, I've also added a few more elements for future forms:

- I am willing to actively participate in the street team challenges on Discord [Yes/No]

- [Title] is classified as "scorching" on the below heat level scale. Are you comfortable with this level of explicit content? [with a graphic showing the varying "heat" levels in romance]
- Please check the platforms where you will leave a review [Amazon, Goodreads, etc.]
- Please link to your most active social media profile
- A thank you message wherein I also give them the option to share the form with their friends

These additions were part of the learning curve I experienced running such a formal street team. Inevitably, there were people who joined and then didn't participate at all, so for future books I wanted to be even clearer that this was the main expectation. While no one commented on the "heat level" of the books, I know that the books get steamier as the series progresses, so I wanted to make it clear exactly what sort of explicit content is on the cards. Checking the review platforms was more for my reference and to remind the readers that cross-posting reviews is encouraged. Asking for the link to their most active social media profile was another measure I put in place to filter out anyone I didn't think was a good match.

Finally, the "share the form" aspect was a happy realisation I had when I saw the sense of community the series starter was fostering. Several of my street team members encouraged their friends to approach me for ARCs or access to the street team. Those readers turned out to be some of the book's biggest fans, sending me screenshots of their live reactions via text to each other, reposting each other's content, etc. So I thought, why not make it part of the official process? If you want to bring a buddy to the street team, the more the merrier!

The recruitment process

So, the form's all well and good, but what do you do with it? How do you get it out into the world and get people on your street team?

I used a staggered approach to gather my team. First (and always first) were my patrons on Patreon. They were the first to get the opportunity to join the street team via the form; it's one of the benefits they receive as patrons – early access to everything I do.

Next, I included the call-out in my newsletter. Again, I was clear that it was an expression of interest, not a guaranteed place on the team. Finally, I posted to social media and included the link to my form in my bio.

I left the form open for several weeks before reviewing the responses. In fact, between us: I actually forgot to close the form even after things had officially kicked off, because, well… life. But that actually worked in my favour in the end, because I did the initial round of acceptances, then realised halfway through the campaign that there were people who had applied after I'd started the promo push. The latecomers were added to my Discord server and managed to breathe new life into the whole community, so it was one of those blessing-in-disguise type errors on my part.

But how did I select who was accepted and who wasn't? For this particular round, I accepted almost everyone because I knew my ultimate goal was to generate that much-sought-after word-of-mouth buzz. I had put questions in place in my form that were designed to flag anyone who wasn't a good fit or might be problematic, so I felt fairly confident with the initial intake of street team members.

Other authors I know use more refined criteria, like X number of social media followers, Amazon reviewers only, etc. However, from what I'd seen in my market research, I knew it wasn't always those with a massive following who moved the dial when it came to spreading the word.

When I had my list of members, I emailed them with instructions on how to join the Discord server and what to expect.

The platform

Authors use various platforms to manage their street teams: Discord, Facebook, Slack, newsletters, etc. I chose Discord because I already used it for my patrons, I had a decent level of familiarity with it and, most importantly, the thought of managing this beast on something like Facebook filled me with dread. I can't stand Facebook for anything organisational – it's messy, things get lost and there's no guarantee people see anything. What I like about Discord (and Slack) is that you can have different channels, essentially categorising topics, which the control freak in me really appreciates.

So, with the platform chosen, I created a Discord

channel called The Laughing Fox, which is a tavern in *The Legends of Thezmarr* series that becomes a bit of an ongoing joke between our main characters. This was a strategic choice, because The Laughing Fox and its sister taverns across the midrealms in the series are an ongoing link between all my books in the *Thezmarr* flagship series world. This means I can use the same server for every launch and street team within that series, and when I do spin-offs (like *Slaying the Shadow Prince*), I can create another server named after the relevant tavern in that series. I currently have two: The Laughing Fox (for *The Legends of Thezmarr*) and The Dancing Badger (for spin-offs from the main series).

What does it look like inside The Laughing Fox? Well, as I mentioned, I like the functionality of having multiple channels. I feel like it helps people stay on track and keeps me sane. Again, this is what works for me – you might find that you want/need something much simpler. You do you. But for those curious, here's a list of the channels:

- Welcome bundle
- Code of conduct
- General
- Media materials
- Weekly challenges
- Ask the author
- Spoiler chat
- Ongoing challenge
- From the author
- Sensitive topics
- Book two WIP teasers
- Socials

. . .

Most of these are self-explanatory, but I want to touch on a few.

First, the "welcome bundle" and "media materials". These channels were specifically designed to give the team members everything they could possibly need to make promoting my book as easy as possible, while also making them feel special and that they were getting benefits the general public weren't.

The welcome bundle included the following (note that all of these items were created at zero cost to me – I was just repurposing content I already had):

- An e-ARC of the book
- A downloadable map
- A visual guide to the midrealms that I created in Canva
- A link to the book's playlist on Spotify

The media materials channel included a link to a Google Drive folder that housed:

- High-res cover images
- 3D images of the book
- An easy-to-copy-and-paste document that includes the blurb, a list of pull quotes from the book, a list of tropes, potential hashtags to use

on social media, and my media kit (more on
that in another chapter)

Again, this channel was designed to make creating content
about the book as easy as possible. Readers didn't have to
scour the book for quotes themselves if they didn't want to
– they had a range to pick from already! They didn't have
to think about what tropes the book features; those were
right there in list form for them to see.

One of the things I've learned about marketing is that
you want to make it as easy as possible for the other people
involved. It shouldn't feel like a huge chore on their list – it
should be a straightforward pleasure to work with you. I
also made a point of asking if there was anything else
participants needed. I made it clear that I was around to
help, and to provide more assets if needed.

The results were fantastic: reels, TikTok videos,
atmospheric aesthetics and such creativity, all surrounding
my book!

Street team challenges

Okay, so you've set everything up, and you've got your team
onto whatever platform you're using... Now what? How can
they help spread the word about the book you're launching?

First, to be clear, I decided on all my tasks and the
rewards I'd be offering *in advance*. None of this was done
on the fly, as I wanted to know exactly what I was offering

and what I was hoping to gain. I had a document that housed what content would be posted each week and which reward would be offered for what challenge.

As I mentioned at the start of the chapter, I decided on a weekly challenge structure. At the start of the week in question, the challenge was posted, along with the prize up for grabs. This was my first challenge:

Week #1

(Do one or all of these tasks to go in the draw for this week's giveaway)

Prize: Paperback of Blood & Steel

Task:

- *Create a graphic including the* Blood & Steel *cover and share it on socials (Instagram & TikTok) along with the book information (release date, pre-order link) — use the hashtag #bloodandsteel and tag @helenscheuerer*
- *Like, share, comment on other street team members' posts — share the love!*
- *Helen will be reposting your content both in her IG stories as well as later scheduled posts*
- *Add* Blood & Steel *on Goodreads if you haven't already*

Winner to be announced before next week's challenge.

Whenever members completed a task, they simply screenshotted it and submitted it to the channel. Each completed task counted as an entry to that week's giveaway, so the more they participated, the higher the chance they'd win the prize.

As I mentioned, there was also an ongoing challenge, which could be participated in at any time over the course of the promotional period. The ongoing challenge was:

- Share your reactions on social media while reading
- Share your progress on Goodreads while you read
- Share the prequel novella

Over the weeks, I included a range of other tasks, such as:

- Post a pull quote on social media from *Blood & Steel* (either of your own choosing, or there are several in the media materials channel)
- Pitch your own idea for promoting *Blood & Steel*
- Tell a friend about *Blood & Steel*
- Like, comment on, share other *Blood & Steel* posts
- Create and post a TikTok or IG reel about *Blood & Steel*
- Create a moodboard or aesthetic
- Join one of the following Facebook groups and recommend *Blood & Steel* in an appropriate thread or leave a public review (where appropriate)

- Share your review of *Blood & Steel* on social media
- Share a countdown post for the *Blood & Steel* launch day (16th)
- Cross-post your review to Amazon and Goodreads (when the book is live)
- Feb 16th – Share a launch day post on IG or TikTok or both! (According to your time zone)
- Post about *Blood & Steel* to a community group you're in, be it Slack/Discord or another Facebook group
- Upvote any five-star reviews on Amazon and Goodreads (this simply means clicking "Yes" to "Was this review helpful?" on Amazon, and "liking" reviews on Goodreads)
- Post an "In Case You Missed It" social media post about the recent release
- Reshare your review on socials

Prizes and rewards

Throughout the whole period, I wanted to maintain the level of excitement as well as the feeling of exclusivity. I also wanted the team members to know how grateful I was for their efforts. In order to do this, I offered a weekly prize, as I described above. Over the course of five weeks, I offered:

- Paperbacks
- A $20 Amazon gift voucher
- A hardcover of the book we were launching

- A complete ebook series from my current catalogue (winner's choice)
- My complete catalogue in ebook format

Yes, some of these were expensive, but I figured it was a small price to pay for the quality of the content these readers were producing for me, and for the power of the word-of-mouth marketing they were creating.

Throughout it all, I was sure to engage directly with my street team members on Discord as much as possible, repost their content, and be vocal about how grateful I was. To keep the engagement up in the server, I also posted teaser snippets from the following book in the series (which I was writing as all of this was going on), replied to comments in the spoiler chat channel, and answered questions in the "ask the author" channel.

A combination of all these efforts made for a very satisfied street team, if I do say so myself.

The wrap-up

The final piece of the puzzle for me was making sure that along with all the engagement and prizes, the team left the promo period feeling like they might want to participate again. So I made sure to leave things on a positive note. I posted a big thank you message in the "from the author" channel detailing how much I appreciated them and how blown away I was by all their support.

Next, I outlined what would happen with The

Laughing Fox between releases. It so happened that my next release was a spin-off and the street team would be run on a sister server (The Dancing Badger). I gave them the opportunity to express their interest in that street team via a new form and mentioned that the cover reveal would be happening soon.

Finally, I didn't want to leave them empty-handed, so I put together a bonus pack for everyone that included:

- A bonus steamy scene
- An exclusive excerpt of my next book (which hadn't been shared anywhere else)

Consider getting help

If you're thinking this sounds like an insane amount of work, you're 100% right. It was. I'm tired just having typed it all out for you. As I started putting it all together, I knew I'd need help. I'm someone who needs to focus on one thing at a time. I can't stand notifications or messages waiting to be answered, and with Discord you can't schedule posts, as far as I know. None of which boded well for my personality type and managing a street team...

At the time, I was in the process of hiring a virtual assistant (VA), but for something this interactive and centred around my books, I felt like this person should be a long-term fan. Many authors I know have fans managing their street teams, so I turned to someone who had been with me since the very beginning and asked if it was something she'd be interested in doing.

Thankfully, she agreed wholeheartedly. I paid her a flat

fee for the five weeks and she took the reins for the whole thing. It was one of the best decisions I've made, and she's since come onboard to manage all my street team endeavours for future launches. (Note: some fans will happily do this task for free. However, I knew the amount of value this particular person would bring to the table would be well worth it, and I had the feeling it might blossom into something more long-term.)

Having a fan do this job made a huge difference. In addition to posting the weekly challenge, managing the drawing of the winners and answering any questions, my street team manager actively engaged with the members, posing her own discussion questions and her own reactions to the group, which fuelled much bigger conversations in the server and contributed to an overall vibe of excitement. She was lovely and encouraging to everyone who participated and cheered everyone on.

Lessons learned

- One thing I hadn't anticipated was the live market research and feedback my street team would provide me with. I was working on the second book in this series as all of this was kicking off, and the live reactions in the spoiler chat channel helped inform some of my decisions about the trajectory of the series. I noticed that some of the most passionate conversations amongst the team were about two side characters who I hadn't planned to feature as much in the upcoming books. However, upon seeing the level of fandom for them, I decided to incorporate them in a much more meaningful way throughout the series. My street team gave me direct insight into what was making readers tick, and I used that to my full advantage to strengthen the series and its marketability.

- In hindsight, the promo period was too long (five weeks), and I felt like people lost steam right up on launch week. I've since adjusted the structure to three weeks: one pre-launch, one for launch week and one post-launch. But this will absolutely depend on the size of your audience and your genre as well.

- Even with someone running the actual event, it was a massive amount of work to set everything up. However, once it was done, I had a framework for all the launches to come.

- Having a clear structure in place in terms of channels, content written in advance and knowing the prizes upfront was a massive help in making everything feel less chaotic.

- Having a street team manager was invaluable. It enabled me to continue on with my actual job of writing the next book, while knowing that this aspect of the launch was in the hands of someone who I not only trusted, but who wanted my books to succeed nearly as much as I did.

TEN

Strategic Pre-Orders for Series Launch

"If you can swing it, pre-orders have a massive number of career benefits, from marketing to productivity to craft. And if you chain them together consistently, you can start seeing pretty rapid compounding across all three areas of your career."
—Nicholas Erik, "Two Launch & Promo Tricks" newsletter

THERE'S a lot of information out there about pre-orders, and a lot of discussion about the pros and cons. But for this chapter, I want to explore how I've used pre-orders as part of a launch marketing strategy and how this has become a staple in my planning for series launches.

As you'll later see in my launch case studies, I didn't utilise a pre-order strategy for the releases in my *Oremere Chronicles* series. Each one was a "live" release (I hit "Publish" when I intended for the book to become available for purchase). However, as I delved deeper into my author career, I realised that this strategy no longer suited me. I wanted to be able to plan in advance and have the links for my upcoming books so I could schedule promotions. I also knew that I wanted to capture those readers who were fresh off the back of a cliffhanger, chomping at the bit for more of the story.

Chaining your pre-orders

I wish I could say I came up with this term, but alas, I'm not that savvy. While I've been implementing the strategy for some time, I first came across the phrase "pre-order chaining" in Nicholas Erik's book marketing newsletter (which you can find a link to in the Resources section). In any case, pre-order chaining is pretty simple. It just means that when you release your current book, you already have the next one available for pre-order.

So for example, when I launched my series starter, *Blood & Steel*, the second book, *Vows & Ruins*, was available for pre-order, and I linked to it in the back of the first book. When *Vows & Ruins* releases, I'll have the next book in the series available for pre-order, and so forth – thus the chain from one book to the next is created.

Author Clare Sager uses this strategy as well: "For later books in a series, I'll always have the pre-order in the back of the book, so that's set for however long it takes."

The benefits of this strategy are plentiful:

- Captures hot leads as they finish the book on a cliffhanger

- Shows the readers you're committed to the series
- Lends an air of excitement to the upcoming release
- Gives algorithms time to learn who to recommend the book to
- Creates an in-built system for launching books in a series
- Gives you the link ahead of release to schedule additional promotion

How I create and manage my pre-order chain

Having done this several times now, I'm pretty pleased with how my pre-order chain works for me. Again, depending on how you operate, you might opt to do things differently. Feel free to cherry-pick what you like from my process and make it work for you.

Here's my step-by-step approach to my own pre-order chain:

1. During the week the final files for the current book are due, set up the next book in the series and submit the pre-order (make sure the series title matches exactly)
2. Once the pre-order is live, get the link and update the back matter of the current book. (Revisit the chapter on back matter if you need, but remember: no chapter breaks, no new pages! Just use a simple ornamental break and "The story continues in…" with the link)

3. I always have the next book's pre-order live upon the current release, but I don't tell anyone just yet. Sure, my more eager readers find it, but with a temporary cover and blurb, I can still make a splash with a cover reveal closer to release. I don't want all that content lost amidst the release of the current book

What do you need in order to do this?

From conversations I've had with authors, many are sceptical about this strategy because they think they need everything to be publication-ready. That's not the case. While I personally like to have the book I'm setting for pre-order drafted, that's just my preference and my stress-inclined nature coming through. The truth is, you actually need very little to create a pre-order besides the title of the next book, the ISBN and your price.

Here's what I do:

- Use a temporary black-and-white cover, ideally with the same series branding and font that will be used on the final cover so it's clear it's all going to match – like so:

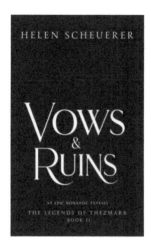

- Use a temporary blurb (sometimes not even that – often my pre-orders just say *"[Character] and [Character]'s journey continues in [Title]. Release date is not final. Release date, cover reveal and official synopsis coming soon!"*). I've seen the temporary cover and blurb strategy used countless times on Amazon by big-name authors like Elise Kova, Carissa Broadbent and Chloe C. Peñaranda
- Update the temporary cover and blurb when I officially reveal the cover
- Always set the pre-order further out than I anticipate the actual release to be – usually by a month or two, more if I'm feeling particularly anxious. This is to provide a buffer if anything should go wrong down the line, whether it's illness, or an editor or designer falling through. It's worth noting, however, that while it's easy to

pull a pre-order forward, delaying the release date/pushing the date back can result in penalisation from Amazon, such as restrictions on future pre-orders. So far, I have consistently moved pre-orders forward (much to my readers' delight) when I'm certain things are ready and in place for a solid launch

Pre-order periods

The question of "the best" pre-order periods has come up time and time again in conversations I've had with authors, particularly those who are newer to the industry. The thing is: the landscape is always changing. For example, there is often talk of the "90-day cliff", the "60-day cliff" and the "30-day cliff" in terms of making the most of Amazon's New Release algorithms. Now, I'm certainly no Amazon expert, but I'm here to share my thoughts and experiences with you, so I'm going to do that now.

For a first book in a series, in my experience, a shorter pre-order period is better for the following reasons:

- A series starter is a new commitment for a reader, an investment, and they might be hesitant to front cash without even being able to use the "Look Inside" feature
- For the same reason, a longer pre-order period might be off-putting if you're an author new to them. It might be a big ask for them to front the cash without any social proof you'll deliver,

or a risk that they'll forget about the release if it's a long way off
- You have a more concentrated chance of hitting bestseller status in your categories
- More and more, readers are wanting instant gratification. It's hard to shell out money for something that won't hit your Kindle for months
- If you're in KU, most KU readers won't pre-order

So, what *is* a shorter pre-order period? In my mind, it's anywhere from 60 days to two weeks.

For a subsequent book in a series, I'm of the opinion that for the most part, the length of the pre-order period doesn't matter, so long as you deliver. This comes back to knowing your rough production rate and streamlining your process so you know what to expect from yourself and can communicate that with your readers. Most platforms currently allow pre-orders for up to a year in advance, which is great news and gives us a fair bit of flexibility.

For example, when *Blood & Steel* launched in February 2023, I had *Vows & Ruins* (book two) up for pre-order with a release date of October 31st. Even as I set this date, I knew full well that I would be launching the book before then (it was already drafted, the cover was already underway and I'd booked my slot with my editor). Originally, I had intended for a July release, but another commitment saw the release date of another title move to that month and I didn't want to launch two books so close together. So I determined that a September release for *Vows & Ruins* would be best. All of this happened behind the scenes without my readers knowing. To their eyes, they'll still be getting *Vows & Ruins* earlier than the expected October date.

Pre-order incentive campaigns

This is something I started to put into place with my second series and have continued to use throughout all my launches since. I've recommended this method to a bunch of indie authors I know who have all implemented it to great effect in their recent launches as well.

In order to encourage pre-orders, I offer an incentive: send your proof of purchase to a designated pre-order email address and receive instant goodies. This helps alleviate some of that need for instant gratification. So far I have offered:

- The first 30 pages of the next book (if it's ready and edited)
- A downloadable goodie, such as a map, a guide or art
- A link to a book playlist

Everyone gets those things instantly. The best thing about this is that it's automated. I create a designated email address for the incentive campaign and then set up an auto-reply from that account. It reads something like:

Hello hello,

Thank you so much for pre-ordering [Title], it means the absolute world to me. As promised, please find your goodies below...

- *The first three chapters of [Title]: link*
- *Your guide to the midrealms: link*
- *The official playlist: link*

Once again, thank you so much for the support.
I can't wait to share this book with you.
Happy reading,
Helen
P.S. Please do not reply to this email. Should you wish to get in touch, the best way is via my personal email address [include regular email address]

From there, I barely lift a finger. Every now and then, just out of curiosity, I'll check that email account to see how many people are submitting or if anyone has missed the part about emailing me directly, but for the most part, I leave it untouched during the months the book is up for pre-order.

What if someone emails the pre-order email address who hasn't actually pre-ordered? My general approach to this is… Who cares? They might get a short story or a playlist, but they were things you're giving away for free anyway and it won't damage your sales.

On launch day or the day after, I gather all the email addresses and send a blanket "Thank you for pre-ordering" email. Depending on what I have on hand, I might also send an additional bonus digital goodie, because I'm a firm believer in "under-promise and over-deliver" and in leaving my most dedicated readers pleasantly surprised.

Previously, I also ran a giveaway as part of this incentive, but it was actually during the research of this book and while talking to author Steffanie Holmes that I realised this might actually be against Amazon's T&Cs in some countries. It's never too late to learn, apparently! I've since dropped this aspect of my incentive strategy and now save the giveaways for other platforms and occasions.

———

Depending on where I'm at in the series, I will also set up my new pre-order incentive for the next book. I have two pre-order email addresses for this reason.

Several of the authors I interviewed for this book do something similar. *USA Today* bestselling author Krystal Shannan told me that one of the most powerful pre-order incentive campaigns she did was a free novella for those who submitted their proof of purchase: "Some of the best pre-order incentives I've done: I've either written a prequel, a couple of chapters… I ran it by my newsletter and said 'If you send me proof of purchase, you'll get the short prequel right now'… and that was the best pre-orders I've ever had in that whole series."

We went on to discuss the beauty of content like this being repurposed down the line as a goodie for your mailing list as well. When I asked Meg Jolly about pre-order incentives, she said: "This is something I LOVE doing and I want to keep doing this to really build the most wonderful reader experience I can. Due to physical constraints around shipping, I usually offer digital incentives. These can be anything from exclusive story material connected to the book launching, artwork of characters/places, or behind the scenes content like mood boards and music playlists."

Of course, some authors offer physical swag as pre-order incentives: things like bookmarks, signed bookplates, postcards, art prints, pens, enamel pins, stickers, etc. If you can afford the production and shipping costs and have the time for all the logistics of a campaign like this, it's a fantastic way to get readers excited about your book. However, as someone who has lived in the middle of nowhere for a while now, these sorts of things just aren't feasible for me, and I'm more than happy with how my digital goodies have worked out so far!

Another strategy I've seen work wonderfully was in two campaigns run by authors Scarlett St. Clair and Danielle L. Jensen. Both authors offered a bonus spicy scene for those who had sent in their pre-order proof of purchase. Instead of delivering this content instantly, however, both authors opted for a release day blast, where all those who had filled out a Google Form with their proof of purchase were emailed the bonus content.

This worked well because it targeted existing fans of both series (*King of Battle & Blood* and *The Bridge Kingdom*). And because you needed to have read the current release to enjoy the bonus content without spoilers, sending it out on release day worked well.

I ended up tweaking this strategy to create a warm reader magnet at the back of my books, but we'll talk about that later.

Final considerations

Rank or bank

This phrase is thrown around a fair bit amongst indie authors when discussing pre-orders. It's the notion that having a pre-order up dilutes your ranking on Amazon. And sure, perhaps your peak rank will be a little lower than it might have been with a live launch, but… you're capturing those sales while they're hot!

I've had long pre-orders that still managed to get those orange bestseller tags, and I've had pre-orders that didn't. You know what? The pre-orders that didn't actually generated more income for me in the long run.

Personally, I'd rather snatch up that sale while the lead is hot.

Deadline stress

Looping back to the whole "we're all different" mentality… Deadline stress is unique to each individual and is definitely something to keep in mind when you're considering using pre-orders as a strategy for launches within a series.

Some people love a deadline as a motivator, some people's creativity dries up under the pressure, and others are somewhere in between. I personally don't like to set a pre-order until the book is at least completely drafted and I can see exactly how its production fits in my timeline. I need to be able to see that there's time for editing, proofreading, getting physical copies and promotion, all with a nice buffer of time to spare in case something goes wrong.

Others will happily set a pre-order without having written a word, and that's just as valid. Again, it really depends on how you react to deadlines and pressure.

Built-in buffer time

I always like to build in buffer time when setting a pre-order date. I ask myself: when is my ideal release date? What could go wrong between now and then? Where is the book currently at in the production pipeline? With those considerations, I pick my "realistic date", and then depending on the other factors, I add up to three months onto that date. So if I want to release in July, I set the pre-order date for October. My intention is always to move the release forward, but life happens… And those three months of buffer time might come in handy down the track.

Knowing I have this time up my sleeve helps me deal with any deadline stress, and if something should happen outside of my control, I've given myself a bit of a safety net.

One pre-order in a series at a time

Personally, I wouldn't have more than one pre-order in a series live unless you plan to rapid release in a big way. Having multiple books on pre-order in your series might confuse readers, and it also unnecessarily decreases the visibility and rank of those later books in the series. So unless you've got a great reason, I'd just stick to one.

Pricing strategy

A brief but important note about pricing: set your pre-order price to the price it will be at launch. The only exception to this is if you're opting for a lower pre-order price and then increasing upon release as part of an aggressive pricing strategy. Do not have a higher pre-order price only to lower it upon release; that's a quick way to piss people off. Also, don't change your mind partway through a pre-order period, because if you set your price for $0.99 and then raise it to $4.99 while still in pre-order, every pre-order will still be charged at $0.99.

ELEVEN

Newsletter Marketing

"One of the best things you can do with a launch is to collect readers who are interested or have read your book and put them in a place where you can easily notify them about future books... That has not changed. The best way to do that is email."
—Steffanie Holmes

WHILE I DON'T CLAIM to be a newsletter marketing expert, I will say that my newsletter list and the content I send my subscribers has played a major role in every launch I've ever done.

This chapter won't tell you how to set up a mailing list or the best platform to use. There are plenty of other books out there that cover this topic in far more depth and technical detail (I'd start with Tammi Labrecque's *Newsletter Ninja*). However, what I *do* want to cover in this chapter is the power of newsletter marketing when it comes to launching the books in your series. I'll be providing my newsletter content strategy for launches and my general approach to my list as a whole. I'll also provide some examples of what I like to include, and how my list and launching strategy has progressed over the course of multiple successful series. Let's get started!

The power of newsletter marketing

I know I'm preaching to the choir here, but bear with me – I'll keep it brief. The power of a newsletter is that it enables you to stay in touch with your readers throughout and in between launches in a way that drives action (sales, reviews, engagement, FANDOM). It is your direct connection to your readers, your main line of communication.

You *own* your list (remember to back it up regularly), so if one of the many social media platforms or even your email provider goes to shit, you've still got your most loyal readers and fans with you.

For me, the best thing about having a newsletter is that it offers readers the opportunity to be part of your inner circle. This is where you share your top-secret news first; where you give behind-the-scenes glimpses of your work in progress. This is where you keep your audience warm and engaged for those upcoming launches.

Other benefits include being able to group and segment particular subscribers; contacting them according to their time zones; using your list to form your team of advanced readers; and, most relevant to this book, having subscribers help you build powerful launch strategies for your series.

The beginning of my newsletter marketing

Like everyone does, I started with a nonexistent platform and zero subscribers when I made the choice to publish independently. I bought Mark Dawson's Self Publishing Formula (SPF) 101 course (admittedly a pricey investment), which helped me understand the sort of foundation I needed to build from the very beginning. I realised I needed an email provider, an automation sequence and a reader magnet, and Mark's course was a great guide, though you can definitely find free information on how to set all this up.

While drafting this chapter, I logged into my old Mailchimp account (I currently use MailerLite) to jog my memory about how this all started for me. It turns out, I sent my first ever newsletter on Friday December 16th, 2016, to a grand total of 10 subscribers. For context, my first series starter, *Heart of Mist*, launched on August 31st, 2017. So nine months ahead of launch, I started my newsletter marketing efforts. Here's what the email said:

It's great to have you on board — welcome.

One of the best things about being an independent author is the direct engagement with my readers.

So, if you want to get in touch, please do. You might have a question about my upcoming book. Maybe you're a fan of [the website I no longer run]. Or you might have a more general question about writing or publishing. Perhaps you've spotted something I could do better.

Whatever it is, please drop me a line. I'd absolutely love to hear from you.

I won't send you updates very often, just when there's exciting news, or new developments I think you might like to know about. I post to my blog a little more frequently, you can check that out by clicking here [blog link]. There's also a nice community of readers over on my Twitter profile, which you can find here [Twitter link].

Thanks again for joining me!

Keep reading, and I'll keep writing.

Until next time,

Helen

It's surreal reading that now, because to be honest, the general tone of my messaging hasn't changed in nearly six years. In any case, I think we can agree that my first newsletter was pretty basic. There's nothing sophisticated about it, and seriously? I didn't even mention "my upcoming book" by name... Oh, how things have changed.

The reason I'm sharing this first newsletter with you is not as an example of stellar newsletter marketing (it's not), but to show you that wherever you're at in your career, you've gotta start somewhere.

I didn't send another newsletter until March 2017. For that, I upped my game. My second ever newsletter was the beginning of an automation sequence – I must have promoted the sign-up link on social media and my blog. It was for the prequels to *Heart of Mist*: short stories I had written as reader magnets to warm up my audience for when my debut series starter released.

From there, I sent a newsletter roughly once a month, and the content of these varied: a cover reveal, another prequel, a monthly recap, a two-weeks-to-launch countdown, a one-week-to-launch countdown (plus a map reveal), a release day blast and a mop-up email a week after.

Over the course of the nine months from my first newsletter to the release day blast, I went from those first 10 subscribers to 846. Yep, I launched *Heart of Mist* to a list of less than 1,000 subscribers. Funnily enough, in terms of content, this is more or less a similar structure to what I use now, only now I email more frequently and to a much larger list.

Which leads nicely into the inevitable question... How do you get newsletter subscribers?

How to get newsletter subscribers

When I first started my list, I got my subscribers via four main methods:

- Giveaways
- Reader magnets (prequel stories)
- A speaking event and a written sign-up form
- Posting to social media (generic "sign up for my book news" call-outs)

These are all still legitimate ways to get subscribers and I still use variations of all of them to this day. Now, there are even more ways to get people on your list. Platforms like BookFunnel, BookCave, BookSweeps and paid services can help boost your subscribers, as can what I refer to as "builders", which involve a bunch of authors paying a fee towards a big giveaway surrounding a comp title or theme. At the end of the giveaway, the organiser will send the "hosts" a list of subscribers who, when entering the giveaway, agreed to sign up for the authors' lists.

However, I've found the most effective way to gain subscribers is by using reader magnets, or as Tammi Lebrecque calls them, "cookies". Essentially, I've used this strategy from the very beginning of my career up to present day because it works so well. The subscribers who sign up via reader magnet forms are quite often the most engaged, and the ones who are most likely to turn into superfans.

I talked about reader magnets in *How To Write A Successful Series* – in fact, there's a whole chapter called "The Power of the Reader Magnet", so I suggest checking that out as well as Tammi's excellent book. But in short, to quote myself: "A reader magnet can be just about anything – a novella, a short story, a character profile, a character interview, fictional police files, a fantasy map, character art. The purpose of this content is twofold: to start building a warm audience by offering potential readers a free trial or 'taste' of your work in exchange for signing up to your mailing list and to reward existing readers of a series who are waiting for the next book."

Essentially, authors can gain new subscribers in a

myriad of ways, but as I launch more books in a series, as I create more "in between" content (bonus epilogues and short stories), my general philosophy is this: build it, and they will come.

Again, this chapter isn't really about managing your list, or building it – it's about marketing *to* your list. So let's get to that, shall we?

How often should I send my newsletter?

When I first started my list, I was only really emailing when I had news, which could mean once a month or every couple of months. Personally, I've found that consistency is key to managing subscriber (and therefore reader) expectations. When I was releasing annually, I found that once a month was enough to stay in touch with my fans and maintain that connection with them.

As I've increased the number of books I write and publish, I've found that I often have more information to share and that I don't want to contain it to one mammoth email. Nowadays, I email twice a month, and more during launch months because I still maintain that technique of "countdown" newsletters.

I also always try to schedule these things in advance. I keep a "Newsletter" label in my Google Calendar and plan months ahead, particularly when it comes to launches, so I know when particular newsletters are going out. After all this time, I have a blueprint of sorts that I use for my launch emails (which I'll share with you in a bit), but the point for me is to make everything as streamlined as possible.

However, it's that old chestnut of figuring out what works best for you. Some authors I know email once a week, others once a quarter; some like to schedule in advance, some like to write on the fly because it feels more organic. As always, it's up to you.

Your regular newsletter content

Before we get stuck into launch content, I wanted to touch on the type of content you can be sending to your list *between* releases. This is content that can keep your readers engaged with you and your work, but that's not necessarily all about directly selling your upcoming title to them.

Steffanie Holmes summed it up perfectly in our interview: "My newsletter is my main way of connecting with people… I always seem to have news to share, but if not I'll share an excerpt of what I'm working on, or I'll tell stories that expand the world for them… It makes the newsletter more than just sell-sell-sell."

So, what can you share? Here are some ideas:

- WIP updates: Where are you at in your writing process? Finished a draft? Finished a particularly harrowing scene? Share your experience
- Teasers: Share a quote from your WIP
- Excerpts or first chapter sample: Share a longer excerpt from your WIP or upcoming book
- Moodboards: Share some aesthetics that match your book

- Playlists: Share what you listen to while writing, or a playlist you created that fits the vibe of your book
- A call-out for questions (and then answers in future emails)
- "Behind the idea": Share how you get your ideas for particular stories; where your inspiration comes from
- Your hobbies (when I was writing *The Oremere Chronicles*, I went horse riding for a week in New Zealand in a very fantasy-esque setting, so I shared that!)
- Setting inspiration (another thing I share regularly because I now live in New Zealand)
- Tease the cover: Book Brush allows you to create graphics that show a partial cover, which are perfect for teasing out the big reveal
- Authors who have inspired you throughout your career
- Book recommendations (both your personal recs and books that are similar to your upcoming title)
- Photos of your workspace (people love a peek behind the scenes)
- Photos of pets (another super popular one)
- Personal announcements (if you're comfortable with this)
- Plans for the future or reflections on the past
- Your writing goals and publishing schedule
- Gift guides with common themes to your book (great for Christmas, Valentine's Day, etc.)

- Sales and promotions of your backlist titles
- Sales and promotions of other authors' titles similar to yours
- Joint sales and promotions with other authors
- Short stories, novellas, bonus or deleted scenes, epilogues, prequels
- Maps, digital artwork, character profiles/interviews
- Interviews that you've done as an author

Launch content for newsletter marketing

As I mentioned above, my "blueprint" of launch newsletters has generally stood the test of time. While I email my list more regularly now, the core structure and timing of these newsletters have rewarded me consistently over the years. For any new release, regardless of its place in the overall series, I send the following emails (or include a segment with this content in a regular email, depending on timing):

- Title reveal/book announcement (if it's a subsequent book in the series, this includes a link to the pre-order)
- Prequel novella (I've done fewer of these over the years, but I always have at least one per series)
- Cover reveal teaser and date of cover reveal
- Cover, blurb and final release date reveal (again, if there's a pre-order link, I'll share this)
- Pre-order incentive (if I'm choosing to do one)

- "One month to go" countdown (this usually includes teaser quotes, any social media buzz, early review quotes, a list of tropes)
- "Two weeks to go" countdown (build the excitement – is this a highly anticipated sequel? Is it the first in a brand-new series?)
- "One week to go" countdown (continue to build the excitement – share five-star reviews, pretty photos, swag, special editions, etc.)
- Launch day blast (*it's out!*, relevant links, more five-star reviews, thank you for support)
- "Mop-up" newsletter (sent a week after release, with a summary of the launch and all the links again in case anyone missed it, and LOTS of gratitude for readers' support)

With the exception of the "countdown"-style newsletters, the rest are spaced out according to my regular newsletter schedule or included in those emails. However, I'd like to focus on two newsletters very specific to launch: the launch day blast and the "mop-up" newsletter.

The launch day blast

Back when I did the SPF 101 course in 2016, there was a series of templates offered for launch emails. I used them with much enthusiasm, grateful that I didn't have to come up with everything from scratch myself. Of course, over the years, my launch emails have evolved to suit me, my readers and the expectations of my genres (epic fantasy, romantic fantasy and fantasy romance).

Below, I'll share with you my own launch day newsletter template. You're welcome to swipe the copy and adapt it to your own release, though I do ask that you don't copy it word for word, more so for the fact that it won't be authentic for *your* readers.

Subject line: It's finally here! [party emoji]

Body copy:
   Hello lovely readers,
   I'm going to try and keep this short and sweet because…
   IMAGE – OUT NOW

[Subheading] Where to get [Title]
   Amazon US [these are generally buttons linked to the relevant Amazon store]
   Amazon UK
   Amazon AUS
   Amazon CA
   Amazon DE

Wherever you are, [Title] will be on your local Amazon store.
   Paperbacks and hardcovers are available on Amazon and should also be available at your favourite retailer.

Remember, the ebook is also available FOR FREE in Kindle Unlimited!

[Button] Grab your copy today!

[Subheading] Thank you

Simple as that, another book goes out into the wild...

I hope with all my heart that you love [Title].

Please feel free to forward this email to any of your friends and family who might be keen to start this new adventure with us.

Last but not least, I wanted to thank you from the bottom of my very full heart.

Your ongoing support means the absolute world to me as I continue to stumble through this epic journey.

I'm so excited that at long last you get to meet [Female Main Character], [Male Main Character] and the gang.

Until next time, happy reading,

[sign-off]

This is a much shorter version of the launch emails I've previously sent, but my thinking is that in the lead-up to launch day, my list has seen all the pictures, reviews, excerpts, the cover, etc. If they're eagerly opening this particular email, they don't need it to be 1,000 words long – they just want the key information, and I want to put as few obstacles in the way of that BUY link as possible.

You may want to include more rave reviews or beautiful bookstagram photos; you may want to include a more personalised thank you – those things are all up to you, so long as the key information of how to get your book is there front and centre.

The "mop-up" newsletter

The term "mop up" is a broader marketing term I picked up a long time ago when I was working as a copywriter for an e-commerce store, but as with a lot of marketing slang, it's just as applicable for author newsletters. All I mean by a "mop-up" email is that it essentially "mops up" anyone who missed the initial launch day blast, or anyone who forgot about it after they opened it and were distracted by work, kids, life, etc.

Here's the general gist of mine:

Subject line: Best launch yet!
Body copy:
Hello lovely readers,
I'm writing this before the morning light has hit my office. It's that pocket of quiet just before the rest of the world wakes up and starts its hustle and bustle, which I absolutely love for writing time, particularly when it's to you guys.
I've got a cup of tea in hand and you might want to grab one too…
You guys… [Title] has been out in the world a

whole week today. Can someone tell me where the time has gone?

[FMC], [MMC] and the whole gang are now out in the world meeting readers, slaying hearts... and wow. They've lived in my head so long it's surreal to think of them finding their forever homes on people's shelves.

From the bottom of my heart, thank you for your comments, your messages, your reviews, your posts on social media and everything in between. I honestly didn't know how this was all going to go, but you, my lovely readers, have gone above and beyond, as always.

A thousand thanks.

[Subheading] A little gift...

A few emails back I mentioned that I was working on a little something for those who read and enjoyed [Title].

Well, here we go... This is a little gift from me to you − a bonus scene from [MMC]'s point of view.

Please note that this is designed to be read after [Title]. It takes a certain steamy scene from [location] and lets us see it from our leading man's point of view.

[Image hyperlinked to BookFunnel download page]

Fair warning: this contains explicit content.

If these bonus scenes are something you enjoy, please let me know by hitting "Reply". One of my priorities this year is making sure I deliver the content readers want, so I'm trying a bunch of new things.

Happy reading!

[Subheading] If you enjoyed [Title]…

I know it's early days yet, but some of you are SUPER fast readers, so with another release done and dusted, it's that time again… Review talk!

Not only do reviews help readers decide if our books are for them, but there are behind-the-scenes benefits too. Amazon algorithms, getting into Also Boughts… The list goes on.

So please, if you enjoyed any of my books, consider leaving a short review on Amazon and Goodreads. It would be an incredible help.

Please and thank you, my bookish friends!

[Subheading] Where to get [Title]

In case you missed it…

Amazon US

Amazon UK

Amazon AUS

Amazon CA

Amazon DE

Wherever you are, [Title] will be on your local Amazon store.

Paperbacks and hardcovers are available on Amazon and should also be available at your favourite retailer.

Remember, the ebook is also available FOR FREE in Kindle Unlimited!

[Button linking to book]

I've had a few questions about the audiobook edition, so I'll address that here too... Currently my agent has it on submission with all the major players, so it's a waiting game at the moment!

The industry has changed a little since my last release and right now, the thing that will really determine if [Title] gets made into an audiobook is the success of the existing editions.

So if you want to see it happen, please help spread the word about the book!

[Subheading] The inevitable question... What's next?

Have I told you guys how much I love this question? I'm a very future-driven person, so I'm ALWAYS thinking about what's next, and what's after that!

I also know this year's release schedule is a little hectic and a little less straightforward than usual, so I want to make sure everyone knows what's happening...

Next up is...

[Image: temporary cover of next release]

[Condensed blurb of the new title]

You can add it to your Goodreads TBR here [link].

I'm so excited to share more with you. Cover reveals and pre-order details to come!

[Subheading] From the writing desk

Well, my lovelies, I'm sure you can imagine what a distracting time it's been during launch week, and as I write this, I'm actually waiting until it's time to pick my family up from the airport...

My parents and sister, as well as my fiancée's mum and brother, are visiting. It's the first time in three and a half years we've seen any family, so we'll be taking a little break to spend some quality time together.

However, I've been hard at work this year already and things will still be ticking along while I'm drinking wine in the mountains! My beta readers are currently reading Book 2 in [Series Title] and my oh my, some of the live reactions I'm getting… Well, I won't spoil things for you, but… let's just say things go up a notch or two from here.

Once we've wrapped up family time, I'll be hitting the ground running with more [FMC] & [MMC], and I quietly can't wait.

[Subheading] And that's a wrap

Well, I'll love you and leave you here folks.

Once again, thank you so much for all your support for [Title].

As always, feel free to hit "Reply" if you've got any questions, or just want to say hi! I really love hearing from readers. It makes this more of a conversation and less like shouting out into the void!

Until next time, happy reading,

[sign-off]

As you can see, my mop-up newsletter was a little lengthier and more personal. It's actually a better example of what my regular newsletters are like. For launch day blasts, I don't like to bog down the crucial information with my tendency to waffle, but on other occasions it actually makes me feel a lot more connected to my readers, and from what I've been told, they appreciate the additional insights.

My general tips for newsletter marketing

Over the years, I've developed my own philosophy about how I approach my newsletter content and therefore marketing. Here are a few takeaways:

- Always under-promise and over-deliver – you'll note that in my mop-up newsletter, I gave my subscribers something for free as a surprise and as a thank you
- Use white space, short paragraphs, dot points, images and headings to break your email up and make it easier to skim (that's how most people read their emails)
- Take note of the subject lines and headings other authors, retailers and services are using in their newsletter marketing and see what works for you (I get inspiration for my subject lines from all sorts of other email marketing campaigns, not just book-related)
- While I don't encourage repeating the same information over and over, don't be afraid to talk about your books regularly

- Experiment with the type of campaign you use for your newsletter sending (e.g. regular campaign, auto-resend, A/B testing)
- When you use an auto-resend campaign, use a personalised message and a new subject line
- Give subscribers the option to sign up for new release news only – some people don't want an email from you unless it's telling them your book is out
- Segment/group subscribers according to how they landed on your list – for example, I have different groups for builders, giveaways, each reader magnet, generic updates and more. This helps to prevent contamination across the engagement of all my groups

Newsletter swaps

Another form of newsletter marketing in the indie author community is something called "newsletter swaps". It's where authors with similar titles in the same genre come together and feature each other in their respective newsletters to cross-promote to each other's audiences.

My experience with newsletter swaps has been a mixed bag. On one hand, it's a great way to connect with other authors in your genre (I've made a few friends from initially cold-emailing them about a swap). Swaps can also be a good way to stagger your promotion before and after a new release or a sale, and to reach a new readership.

Personally, however, I've found them to be a lot of work. There's the initial creation of the list of authors you'd like to reach out to, not to mention the umming and ahhing over whether or not you're at a similar career level (both list size and sales-wise), and whether they'll reply or think you're annoying; then comes the actual drafting and sending of the initial emails, management of replies and coordination of the swaps themselves.

Right now, I have a go-to list of authors I've worked with in the past who I trust, and I've currently got my VA compiling a list of "dream authors" I'd like to work with in this respect, but we'll see how that goes.

For the most part, swaps make up a very small part of my newsletter marketing now. This is partly a personal thing – I don't like reaching out to people I've never spoken to, I don't like the fiddly aspect of managing all the moving parts, and I've been burned a few times by authors who haven't delivered, or who have been misleading about the quality and size of their list. I also know that swaps can be dependent on the genre you're in, so the best advice I have in this respect is to do your research. What are your comp authors doing? What's working for your peers in your genre? Start there.

––––––

As you can see, there's a lot to play with when it comes to newsletter marketing, and ultimately, your list and content can be a powerful tool in your launch strategy for all the books in your series.

TWELVE

Content Marketing

"I go extremely hard on social media, really pumping the messaging out there. This comes easy for me because I am genuinely hyped about my books and I love sharing things about them with my readers! I've found that getting extremely excited, sharing lots of teasers, etc. has really put jet-fuel in my launches far more than anything else."
—Carissa Broadbent

CONTENT MARKETING IS another one of those terms that gets thrown around a lot, but when asked, a lot of us find it hard to define. When I'm talking about content marketing, I'm mainly talking about the online space, so we'll keep the conversation there for the purposes of this chapter.

The thing is, most of us are already implementing a variation of content marketing in our strategies without realising it: creating and publishing content for the purpose of driving leads to our books. It's natural to share stuff about what we're working on, right? That's content marketing.

The content we create for marketing purposes can be written or visual and for just about any platform. It includes graphics, videos, blog posts, infographics, reels, TikTok videos, tweets, social media content in general, newsletters (though we'll keep those to the previous chapter to keep things tidy), podcasts, interviews and just about anything in between.

The purpose of content marketing isn't the same as something like paid advertising, which is to result in a direct return on investment (ROI), but rather to increase brand awareness, educate an audience, encourage conversations and build relationships with your readers over time, all of which essentially funnel into a community of sorts.

Now, were this book solely focused on this topic, we might delve deeper into how you can split the various types of content marketing into different subcategories, but for the purposes of our author businesses (and sanity), let's keep it simple.

The content marketing woes of a fiction author

One thing I'll say is that I've found it much easier to do content marketing for nonfiction books than for fiction books. A nonfiction book answers a question or solves a problem, whereas a fiction book entertains. It's far easier to pitch a podcast with "Hey, I'll talk about how to launch a successful series" as opposed to "Hey, I'll talk about my latest romantic fantasy release". However, that's not to say it's impossible; you just need the right tools and approach.

Below, I'll explore the different types of content you can create to post on your own platforms. However, a big part of content marketing is actually creating content for other people's platforms – for example, writing a guest post for someone's blog, or being featured on a YouTube channel. For the most part, these opportunities don't just fall into an author's lap – they're a whole other kettle of fish that we'll explore in the chapter on outreach marketing. This definitely has some crossover with content marketing, but there are some specific steps I want to delve into, so you'll find more on this approach in that chapter.

For now, I want to focus on the kind of content you can produce for your own platforms.

A steady drip of content

First, I want to make something clear: I'm not sitting here telling you that you need to post to Instagram or TikTok or whatever the latest new platform is every day. Believe me, I get how draining it can be to have to create *more* content on top of the actual books you're writing, the blurbs you're creating and all the rest. However, part of being an indie author is not only the writing and publishing of your books, but the marketing of them as well. And that's where this type of content comes in.

The platforms you choose to focus on and how often you share content is completely up to you. This will depend on a lot of factors, including how often you release, whether you've got other things to manage like a family or a day job or a chronic illness, etc. It'll depend on how much you have left in the tank before, during and after you've written the actual book, and of course, the platform itself will depend on where your readers generally hang out.

However, here's what I've done over the years throughout my launches in terms of content marketing. I've chosen the platforms I'm most comfortable on: Instagram and my newsletter, with a more recent dipping of the toes into TikTok.

I lean on a few things:

- A list of general content ideas appropriate to my audience/genre
- A list of launch content that I recreate with each release
- A content calendar to keep me organised

One of the keys is not to use every post as an opportunity to promote/sell your book or upcoming launch, but to stay in the general vicinity of your genre and what your audience is interested in. For example, my list of general content includes a bunch of "Questions of the Day" (#QOTD), which I can post as a caption alongside either a generic picture of pretty books, or one of my own books so that I'm getting it in front of people, but engaging them about a linked topic, not actually asking them to buy my book.

Some examples of the general/generic content I post alongside pretty book images are:

- What was the last book you read?
- Where is your favourite spot to read?
- What's your favourite genre?
- How did you get into reading?
- Series or standalones?
- How do you arrange your bookshelf?

Then there's content that's specific to me, but not quite attempting to directly sell my books:

- FAQs (about a series, author life, general questions in my inbox)
- Anniversary posts (e.g. *Heart of Mist* turns six, five years since we said goodbye to *The Oremere Chronicles*, etc.)
- Gratitude post (thanking authors, friends, etc. for help when struggling)
- Author update (what I've been working on)
- Desk/behind the scenes (usually snapshots of how messy my desk is mid-draft)
- Announcements
- Quarterly plans/goals
- To do lists

Then, there's the launch content I tweak and recycle for every launch...

- Book quotes
- Cover coming soon
- Cover reveal teaser
- Cover and blurb reveal
- Prequel announcement (if applicable)
- Prequel quotes
- Prequel launch
- Moodboard – aesthetic/vibe of upcoming book
- Thanks to cover reveal team (+ repost other accounts' images with credits)
- Map teaser
- Opening line
- Teaser quotes from the book
- One month to go
- Three weeks to go
- Two weeks to go
- One week to go
- One more sleep
- Sale/promo of first-in-series (if applicable)
- Early reviews
- "Themed" regular post, e.g. #FridayFeels (emotional book quotes or questions)
- Shelfie with the new book (people love seeing your actual bookshelf, and your face for that matter)
- Reveal of hardcover interior
- Unboxing video – paperback

- Unboxing video – hardcover and naked cover (these do particularly well in my genre)
- Character art (if any)
- Promoting upcoming Instagram/TikTok Live events
- Launch nerves (sharing how you're feeling with your community often goes a long way)
- Full map reveal
- Calm before the storm (launch week)
- Launch day post (AM)
- Launch day post (PM)
- Launch update (next day) – any bestseller tags, more thanks, more reposting images
- How we're celebrating launch
- With every release, recreate selfie "stack" photo with all published books – people love to see your catalogue grow!
- Next book title coming soon
- Next book title announcement and up for pre-order
- "One week on" update
- Launch week gratitude
- Total words published (with stack of all books)

Both the general content and launch content are housed in a spreadsheet I call my "content pool". It eliminates overwhelm and decision fatigue for me when I sit down to create content for social media and newsletters.

In *How To Write A Successful Series*, I talked about the

importance of market research… and in my more recent series launches, the crucial nature of this step has become more and more apparent to me. If you do your market research before and during the writing process, you'll find that you actually bake in marketable elements throughout your story, which makes content marketing *so much easier.*

This realisation led to me adding a new step to my own editorial process. As I edit/read my work, I mine it for "pull quotes" or hooks: solid gold content for social media. Basically, whenever I come across a mic-drop quote or a brief scene that encompasses a popular trope, I copy it into a document that I creatively title "Book Title Pull Quotes". I now keep a document like this for each book so that when it comes to creating content, I'm not drawing a blank trying to remember things off the top of my head or having to reread a 130,000-word book for a single quote.

Carissa Broadbent shares her wisdom here, and it's something that's stayed with me:

> *"I think that far and away the thing that matters the most about a launch and book marketing in general is A) writing a book that people will LOVE LOVE LOVE, B) knowing exactly what people LOVE about that book and C) articulating B in a snappy way that resonates with your audience. In practice, these things are not as simple as they sound – many authors (myself definitely included) don't start out actually knowing in very specific terms why readers love their books, because a lot of times what they love and what we love are not a 1:1 match. It's also hard to figure out where your audience lives and what language resonates best with them. However, once you figure those things out, I fully believe it is the only thing that matters."*

Scheduling your content

As you can see from the lists above, which only scratch the tip of the iceberg when it comes to your content options, there's a fair bit to manage. Personally, I can find it overwhelming at times, so I need a system in place to help me keep things in order. However, there will be authors out there who prefer to post content as they think of it, or as they have a spare moment waiting for the kettle to boil. Whatever your preference, go for gold.

However, for those who want to be able to "set and forget" at times, scheduling might be a good option for you. I am a big fan of scheduling content. I'd schedule the whole year in advance if I could.

Over the years I've used a few different tools for this: Buffer, Hootsuite and currently a platform called Onlypult, but there are loads out there all with different features and functionalities, so it's best to do your research depending on the channel/s you're hoping to schedule content for. (I feel incredibly frustrated that there's no decent option for scheduling TikToks weeks and months in advance yet.)

I'll be forever refining my processes as I learn new things and new tools become available, but currently I use Google Calendar to map out my content for the upcoming month, depending on where I'm at in the launch process. Once I know the launch date of a book, I tend to work backwards, using my launch content list to make sure that I'm not missing anything crucial and that I'm putting the "countdown" style posts on the right days. This gives me a skeleton to plan my more general content around, and I also try to remember to share content related to my backlist titles as well (though this gets increasingly hard the more books you have out).

How often you post is completely up to you. When I'm not in full-on hype mode for an upcoming release, I try to keep it to three or so posts per week on Instagram, but when I'm ramping up for a launch, I'll post every day, and during launch week often twice a day. You might post more or less often, depending on your needs and circumstances.

———

In my interview with Krystal Shannan, we talked about the different seasons of life and how they affect our launch strategies and careers in general. You don't always have the same amount of fuel in the tank, and no launch is going to be the same as the last, no matter how much you try to duplicate the results. For me, that applies to content marketing and the content I'm trying to produce in addition to my actual books. Content marketing is my way of staying connected with my readers and keeping them in the loop, particularly in between releases in a series.

THIRTEEN

Outreach Marketing

"Where readers hang out [online] is always going to vary depending on what genre you are. Mystery readers hang out in different places to fantasy readers, etc. People of different ages hang out in different places... The readers will move around different platforms... [We] as the authors have to be quite agile and follow them around."
—Steffanie Holmes

AHH, there are so many moving parts to a launch, aren't there? For me, outreach marketing has always been a big part of the puzzle. But what is it? Essentially, outreach marketing is where you "reach out" to other people with platforms or channels in your designated field or genre to feature you and/or your book. This can include podcasts, YouTube channels, blogs, and traditional media like magazines, newspapers and TV shows. I tend to include influencers in this category as well, because unless you're using a tour service (more on those in the chapter on paid promotion), you're still doing the labour of compiling a list, emailing with a pitch of sorts and managing things from there.

And there you have the crux of it: pitching. You are pitching yourself and your work to others in the hopes that you might gain access to their audience and exposure for your book.

How do you find people and platforms to pitch to?

Don't hate me for saying this, but this is where a lot of your initial market research comes back into play. If you did this upfront, you might be aware of where your comp authors are being featured – you might listen to genre-based podcasts or subscribe to online publications in your niche, or you might already have a list of dream BookTokkers to contact. Those are your first port of call. However, if you didn't do that research, or things have changed, there's still a way.

When I've exhausted all my initial research (or back when I was a newbie and hadn't done any), I do what I like to call "reverse engineering" sources. So for example, I would search for "Sarah J. Maas interviews" or "Elise Kova interviews" from within the last year and read through the results. From there, I'd go to a blog's website and check that they accepted requests from authors.

With the decline of bookish blogs and a move towards TikTok, I essentially do the same thing there. I type a relevant comp title, trope or genre in the search bar and sift through the creators there who are loving the sort of books I'm writing and publishing.

My original outreach marketing spreadsheet has separate sheets for reviewers, Instagrammers and BookTubers, all with the following information:

- URL
- Contact name
- Email address
- Type of content (review, guest post, interview)
- Notes (for any details regarding review policies or expectations like physical copies)
- Number of followers/traffic (to their blog – there used to be a plugin/extension to swipe this info easily)
- Date contacted
- Response
- Book format
- Copy sent
- Follow-up 1
- Follow-up 2
- Content due
- Live link
- Live link 2
- Cross-posted to Amazon?
- Cross-posted to Goodreads?

The spreadsheet I'm working with at the moment is a variation of this that my assistant and I now use as a team.

When I first started preparing my launch plan for *Heart of Mist* in 2017, book blogs were very influential and much more popular than they are now. At the time of writing this, TikTok is currently the major player in terms of where influencers are, so I've pivoted a lot of my outreach marketing focus there. You'll hear more about those strategies in my launch case studies. But the point is, having these systems and strategies in place makes it easier to pivot when things change.

Media kits

So, you've got your list of platforms/people/influencers you want to reach out to – now what? The main thing I want to address in this chapter is something that I've found incredibly useful since day dot: media kits. A media kit (or press kit) is a set of materials that provides core information about a product or business to journalists and the media in general. A decent media kit houses all the vital facts about a product (in our case, a book), while also making it easy for the media to write about it.

Over the years, I've taken great pride in creating a professional-looking media kit for every single one of my books and sending it out to bloggers and influencers. I make it as easy as possible for them to feature me. I include graphics they can use, the book's blurb, review quotes, even a list of questions so they don't have to come up with content themselves if they choose to interview me. I've used the same blueprint time and time again, tweaking and amending its design. Only recently I thought to add tropes and pull quotes for social media, making it even easier for others to create content about my book.

On the first page of my kit, I list what it includes. That list looks like this:

- Book synopsis
- Book details, comparative titles & tropes
- Cover reveal (often under embargo)
- Book excerpt (usually the first page or so of the book)
- Pull quotes for social media
- Introducing the free prequel (what it is, where you can get it)
- Praise for my catalogue of work
- Author bio
- Interview, article and guest post topics
- Contact details

In the "Bonuses" section of this book, I'll include a link to one of my media kits so you can see it in action and potentially use it as a starting point for designing your own.

I think these kits lend an added element of professionalism to a pitch, and are a great way to present all the vital info about your book in one pretty place. Since the beginning, I've used Canva to design mine and it has worked like a charm. To me, the point of a media kit is not only to attract a potential reader, but also to make it as easy as possible for them to feature you on whatever platform they have.

The best part? I use my media kits for more than just outreach marketing. I also send them to:

- Potential reviewers
- Tour promotions I'm booking
- My agent (to pitch to audiobook and foreign language publishers)
- Fellow authors with whom I want to join forces

The pitch

Depending on who I'm approaching, the pitch changes slightly, so bear that in mind with the template below. It's also worth noting which book in the series you're pitching. For example, for a dynamic/sequential series (i.e. one with an overarching story arc that continues across multiple books), I only pitch book one to those who are new to my work, because there's no point trying to hook them on book two as they won't know what's going on. I only pitch the subsequent books to people who have already read the previous instalments. I do, however, continue to pitch book one to new influencers throughout the launches of the later books in order to reach new audiences for the series.

If you write episodic series or interconnected standalones, there's a little more freedom to how you can pitch your books with each launch, as each one could potentially be an entry point to your series, with no previous reading required.

I try to personalise my pitch to the platform or influencer where possible. But the general gist of it is the following:

. . .

Hi [Name],

I hope you don't mind me reaching out. My name is Helen Scheuerer, I'm the author of the upcoming romantic fantasy series starter, [Title], which I'm launching on [date].

I'm currently looking for BookTokkers who enjoy the genre to help spread the word.

You can check out the media kit here: [link]

If you're interested in receiving a paperback/hardcover copy, do let me know, I'd love to send you one for review or feature.

If you have a rates card, I'd love to see it.

Hope to hear from you soon :)

Thanks for your time,

Helen

Obviously, the more personalised the better. When I'm doing my outreach marketing research, I make sure I'm following anyone I intend to contact. I'll also make a note of anything helpful in the notes section of my spreadsheet – things like if they have a favourite author, or if they do a series of videos on a particular topic that might be useful for my pitch.

––––––

Outreach marketing has always played a significant role in my launches, and as you can see, it's a lot of work on top of everything else. However, the rewards have certainly been worth it for me. Additionally, the beauty of a series is that after the initial work of forming relationships with influencers for book one, you have a blueprint for those you'll want to contact for the next launch in the series (provided they liked and reviewed/featured the first book, of course).

FOURTEEN

Paid Promotion

"I make my money from the long game."
—Krystal Shannan

SO FAR, the majority of the launch strategies and marketing we've covered has been at little to no cost to the author (besides their time and energy). However, there are of course a range of paid services and tools that authors can use to bolster their launches and their general marketing of a series. We're going to cover those in this chapter.

Before we dive in, there are a few things to consider. First, before signing up for a bunch of services or booking slots with all the promo sites, I encourage you to examine where you are in your career, where you are in the series you're marketing, and your own expectations as to the return on investment you're hoping to get. For example, is this your first book in a series, or your first book ever? Is it a change in genre? Do you have something in the pipeline to follow it up with? There's no point in making a loss on book one if you can't recoup your costs on the sale of book two.

Krystal Shannan makes the distinction between spending time and spending money on a launch. With the release of a new series starter on the horizon when we spoke, she explained that she's happy to spend time on social media and talking about the book, but that she won't invest money in advertising on a book one, "because it doesn't have anything behind it yet". She went on to explain, "I make my money from the long game," which is a mentality that a lot of successful indie authors share, myself included.

Over the years I've become a lot more intentional about where in a series I spend the bulk of my money. I'm the opposite to Krystal in that I like to make a splash with book one (as well as the final book), but similarly to Krystal, I reserve spending my budget on advertising until more of the series is out.

Never go into debt for book promotion or advertising – that's pretty standard advice across the board. We're all guilty of getting overexcited and wanting to throw everything at a launch, or alternatively, panic-booking a bunch of things in the hopes that something we throw at the wall will stick. More often than not, both approaches result in disappointment.

The other thing to note is that if you have the "spaghetti at the wall" approach, you won't actually be able to tell what worked and what didn't for next time. The key to figuring out how to make paid promotion work for you is a lot of trial and error, and experimentation. As with most things in this industry, what works for one author may not work for another, so it's up to you to do your genre and market research and play around with the options until you discover the pieces of your own puzzle.

We want to be strategic in the paid promotion we explore for our series, and the best way to do that is to experiment on a smaller, staggered scale before levelling up and adding to our foundation. So, with that said, what are the options?

Paid advertising

The big gun of paid promotion is advertising. I'm talking about platforms like Amazon's AWS Managed Services (AMS), Facebook and BookBub, to name the heavy hitters.

If you're thinking about starting paid advertising on your series, I strongly suggest taking a look at what your comp authors are doing. Where are they focusing their efforts? What seems to be working? What platforms are they using?

Don't know how to work out who is advertising where? At the time of writing this, it's simple enough to find out. For Amazon, search the site for your chosen comp author or the genre you're in. From there, you'll be able to see in the results what/who is marked as "sponsored", which means the spot on the results page is paid for.

For Facebook, go to your comp author's page (official page, not personal profile) and click "About". From there, under their contact information is "Page Transparency", where you'll be able to see "This Page is currently running ads" (if they are doing so). If you click "See All", you'll be shown a bunch of options, including "Go to Ad Library". Click this and you'll be taken to a content library of the ads they're running and have run in the past on Facebook. You'll be able to see when the ad started running, the platforms it's running on (Facebook, Instagram, Messenger, etc.), and whether it has multiple versions. You will be able to see the written ad copy as well as the images used and the general structure. It's incredibly valuable information for your own ad research.

For BookBub, you can sign up to the newsletters in your genre and see what books are chosen as their Featured Deal (those authors were selected for a Featured Deal and paid for the spot). You can also scroll down and see the ad at the bottom of the newsletter to determine which comp authors are using CPM (cost per mille – click per thousand impressions) paid advertising.

While I certainly don't claim to be an expert on any of these, I've dabbled with all of them since I started publishing. For the most part I've chosen to concentrate on AMS. Over the years I've learned that advertising is not something I enjoy or feel I'm particularly good at, and as such, I've outsourced this task in the past and I hope to do so again in the future. This is a controversial move in the indie author community, as there are camps of people who insist that no one can know your book better than you, and that if you pay someone, you're giving away half your profit or more to pay for those services.

Personally, I know myself well enough by now to know that I'm never going to give advertising my all, because I don't enjoy it. I struggle to understand the finer details and I lack the patience for the ongoing tasks of managing ads; therefore, even if I'm investing in advertising, I know I'm not the best person for the job and that I'm potentially leaving money on the table, or even wasting money, by doing them myself.

———

I'll share some resources for paid advertising shortly; however, one more thing I will note is the importance of understanding your own read-through/sell-through rate. This comes up time and time again in books and courses on this subject, and for good reason. A lot of paid advertising works on the assumption that the first book in a series can act as a loss leader (a book sold at a loss in order to attract readers to the subsequent books). Of course, this means you have to have more than one book out, as well as know the conversion rate of readers from book one to book two and so forth.

Knowing your read-through rate adds to the value of the sale of book one because you can determine what you're willing to spend/lose on those ads for the first book, while expecting a profit on the overall series sale (this is the beauty of launching in series). With a good read-through rate, you have a lot more flexibility to experiment with those initial ads, which is great because setting up ads on any platform is a trial-and-error situation. (For more on read-through and sell-through rates, see Chapter 24.)

———

As I said, I'm by no means an expert on paid advertising for books. However, it can be a fantastic strategy for many authors, both on launching and throughout the course of their career. So, here are some in-depth resources that might help:

- *Amazon Decoded: A Marketing Guide to the Kindle Store* (Let's Get Publishing Book 4) by David Gaughran
- *Help! My Facebook Ads Suck*: Second Edition (Help! I'm an Author 1) by Mal Cooper
- *Self-Publishing with Amazon Ads: The Author's Guide to Lower Costs, Higher Royalties, and Greater Peace of Mind* by Bryan Cohen
- *Amazon Ads for Authors: Tips and Strategies to Sell Your Books* by D. M. Potter
- *BookBub Ads Expert: A Marketing Guide to Author Discovery* (Let's Get Publishing Book 3) by David Gaughran

Paid newsletter promotion

For those who are unfamiliar with paid newsletter promotions, these are essentially book deal sites that send out newsletters with said deals to a large subscriber base. Authors pay these sites a fee to feature their books, usually at a discount (most commonly $0.99 or free).

At the time of writing this book, some popular sites are Robin Reads, Fussy Librarian, Ereader News Today (ENT), Bargain Booksy and Freebooksy, to name a few. Luckily for us, David Gaughran publishes an updated list on his blog annually, where he includes the best sites according to best value for money, and sites specific to particular genres.

I highly recommend checking out his blog and signing up for his mailing list, and also taking his free Starting From Zero course, which shows you how to leverage these promo sites for a long tail of success during your launch periods. It was actually this course that helped me refine my own price promotion and launch strategies throughout my series, so my methods are modelled closely on what David explores. You'll find the link to the course in the Resources section.

Here's a snapshot of my strategy…

- Launch book one at full price
- When book two and/or three launches (depending on the time between releases), price book one at $0.99 and book a bunch of promo sites. The idea is that I'm driving new traffic and potential readers to the $0.99 first book and hopefully feeding them into the sales funnel of the entire series
- Upon release of the final book, price book one at free in "celebration" of the completion of the series and book the promo sites specific to *free* books, again driving new traffic to book one and potentially hooking new readers into the funnel
- Whenever I'm booking these promo sites, I never book them all on the same day. I stagger them out across the week that I'm doing the

price promotion in order to create a longer tail of sales rather than one initial spike, which is much better for the Amazon algorithms

It's also worth mentioning BookBub in this section in reference to their Featured Deals (not their ads). Similarly to the sites above, this service emails a list of readers (often in the millions) with a curated list of discounted ebooks segmented by genre. The thing with BookBub Featured Deals (BBFD) is that they're chosen by a team of editors – you have to apply for one and it's quite rare to be accepted, especially if you're in KU.

To give you some perspective, I've been applying since I started publishing in 2017. At first I did so quite sporadically, but now it's on my monthly to do list: "Apply for BookBub". I've lost count of how many times I've applied by now, but I've only ever been accepted once and that was for an International Deal (not US-based, where most of my audience is). It wasn't nearly as effective or lucrative as I had expected. And that's something else to note: a BBFD doesn't come cheap. The pricing depends on your genre, but it's in the hundreds-of-dollars range.

Book tour services

Another form of paid promotion that has grown in popularity over the years is paid book tour services for platforms like Instagram, TikTok and blogs. There are actually dozens and dozens of these services currently available, but more often than not, they're a mixed bag, and having used them for several launches across two different series now, I can report mixed results.

I don't want to recommend particular tours because they change all the time, but what I would suggest is searching for "Instagram book tours" or "TikTok book tours" to see what the most recent results show. From there, it's all about digging deeper to see if they're a suitable service for you. For example:

- What genres do they promote?
- What's the engagement like on the posts they're sharing?
- What authors are they sharing and are any of these authors relevant to you and your work?

You may also find that some of these tours lean more heavily into one genre than others; for example, fantasy romance is hugely popular in this particular community.

The tough thing with these services is that you'll have a hard time measuring the ROI in terms of actual sales. How I approach this element of marketing is by thinking of it more in terms of creating brand awareness and getting your book in front of potential readers – getting them to add it to their TBR on Goodreads and sparking conversations about the cover, for instance.

Some things to be mindful of: some tours require the author to send physical copies to hosts, which can get very expensive. For many of the review-style tours, the hosts partaking aren't actually *required* to write reviews, which can result in some very similar generic content posted over and over again. In addition, the quality of the imagery isn't guaranteed, so it can be a very mixed bag – some photos are simply stunning, while others leave a lot to be desired.

One thing I have *loved* about using these services, however, is that when the content is good, it's *beautiful* (it helps to have a stunning cover, by the way). In my experience, any one tour can produce dozens of images that I can then save and reshare on my own platform at a later date (crediting the original poster, of course). It has actually become part of my strategy whenever I do a cover reveal or a launch to block out some time not only to reply to the creators and thank them for their beautiful photos, but to save the images in a folder (using the handle of the creator as the file naming convention so I can tag them later). This way, whenever I need to schedule my social media content and I need a pretty picture of my book, I've got a whole library full of them, and thanks to the naming convention, I know who to tag and credit in my post. Thanks to the tours I've done over the years, I've actually got months', if not years' worth of content I could schedule, which is fantastic because it's one less thing for me to master (book photography is not a strong suit of mine).

All in all, when it comes to these tour services, it really depends on your budget, expectations and launch goals, but they're a great option to consider.

Organised author giveaways

I'm seeing more and more of these types of promotions going around, where a group of authors come together to offer a joint prize pack, usually a bunch of paperbacks or hardcovers linked by theme. So for example, it could be seven paperbacks that all feature the "enemies to lovers" trope, or seven hardcovers that all feature the word "court" in the title. However they're linked, it's the authors who are paying for the cost of the books and shipping, and any advertising behind the campaign should they choose to run ads via Facebook or Instagram.

The purpose of these sorts of giveaways can be to gain followers or email addresses, but ultimately they leverage the audiences of the authors involved, with each author sharing to their platform, be it their social media pages and/or their newsletter.

These sorts of promotions can be hit or miss. I've only been in a handful and none of them have moved the dial for me in terms of followers or sales, for the most part. However, I will say that you need to trust the authors involved to do their part, both in the sharing required and then the sending out of prizes. Just something to note!

———

As you can see, there are loads of options when it comes to paid promotion, and the beauty is that they don't have to be contained to launches alone. Many can be used again and again throughout a book or series' lifetime to breathe new life into that sales funnel.

FIFTEEN

Price Pulsing and Discounts in Your Series

"Promo sites are basically like Groupon for ebooks: authors pay a fee to have their book listed in the daily offers – usually sent out by email – and they get lots of sales or downloads in return. Readers get freebies and discounts, and the author's book jumps into the charts; everyone wins."
—David Gaughran, "Best Book Promotion Sites in 2023"

ONE THING I love about releasing books in a series is that it provides you with ongoing promotional opportunities. As an indie author, you are the one in control of your pricing strategy. You have the ability to decide when and if you offer discounts, as well as how these are staggered throughout the releases of the books in your series.

Let's talk about a few options…

Permanently free or discounted book one

Many authors utilise the strategy of having book one in their series as a loss leader (pricing it at either free or $0.99) in order to cast the net as wide as possible in terms of gaining an audience for their series. This aggressive pricing removes the barrier to entry for many readers, eliminating or minimising the risk of paying for something they might not like.

This style of pricing is called a "loss leader" because authors generally lose money on that first book in the form of advertising, as well as the fact that they're not earning an income on that title to earn back the money they put into its production. However, with a series, that money can be recouped if the reader goes on to read the subsequent books. If the series is a long one, even better. For a strategy like this, tracking your read-through and sell-through rate is crucial to understanding how sustainable your loss leader is, but I'll cover series read-through rates in the FAQs chapter.

Many authors have found success using this method, including David Gaughran, Elana Johnson and Mark Dawson; all have credited a loss leader to the success of a series at one time or another. The interesting thing about authors who utilise this strategy is that they use it in conjunction with a range of other techniques. You'll often see that only *some* of the first books in their series are priced so aggressively, in addition to a combination of the other strategies below.

Free or discounted book one launches

This was the pricing strategy I used for the launches of each book in my first series, *The Oremere Chronicles*. It was an aggressive tactic, but it paid off in spades. When *Heart of Mist* came out, I "live"-launched it and priced it at $0.99 for a week, then $2.99 the week after, before it went to full price at $4.99 (more on this in the chapter on its launch case study). I utilised a few paid promotion sites, though back then there weren't nearly as many as there are now.

For an unknown author, this was a great way of getting in front of new readers and removing that price point as a barrier to entry for the series. I used this pricing strategy for each book in *The Oremere Chronicles* before launching my next series at full price.

Limited time sales

We're all aware of the lure of a "limited time only" sale. There's an instant adrenaline spike as we consider whether or not we want to miss out on such a deal. This strategy has been used over and over again in publishing to great effect. It could be a price promotion at half-price of the RRP, $0.99 or free – again, you're in control, and as always, you should look at what's working for other successful authors in your genre. The key here is that this promotion is for a limited time only. It may be a weekend, it may be a week, but when pushing this promotion, you want to emphasise the limited time nature of the deal.

Price pulsing and launches

Now *this* is my favourite method of the bunch, and is largely modelled on the advice given by David Gaughran in his free Starting From Zero course, which I highly recommend. I've been using this method for my past two series and it's worked a treat. Essentially, I always price new releases at full price (including book one), which allows me the flexibility to discount them further into the series.

Here's what I do...

- Book one launches at full price ($4.99)
- Book two launches at full price ($4.99) and I assess whether I want a sale of book one to bring new readers into the series funnel. If so, I price book one at $0.99 "in celebration" of book two's release
- Book three launches at full price ($4.99) and if I didn't offer a sale of book one in the last release, I do that now for $0.99

I generally don't discount a book until six months after its initial release, as I don't want to upset those loyal readers who paid full price for it, but for me it's usually about six months between releases anyway. If I'm releasing closer together, I'm more discerning about the number of price promotions I do. Depending on how long the series is and how long between releases, it goes on like this. Sometimes,

I'll discount book two, again depending on where we're at in the overall series release schedule, but more often than not, it's just book one in the series, as I write dynamic/sequential series (those that need to be read in order) and that's where readers have to start.

Usually, I save the big free promotion of book one until the launch of the final book in the series. I want this to make a big splash, and targeting freebie seekers for the first time in the series' lifetime is a great way to do this. They're a different kettle of fish to even the $0.99 discount hunters, so it can be really effective to save this card for last for maximum impact.

When I'm price pulsing and discounting books in this fashion, I'm sure to utilise paid promotion sites like Fussy Librarian and Robin Reads (I've included David Gaughran's excellent list of these sites in the Resources section of this book). I'll keep book one discounted for the launch week of the current book and stagger a bunch of newsletter promotions around it, as well as promoting the sale via social media and my newsletter with a CTA along the lines of "Now's a great time to start the series for free/$0.99". Anyone who has been on the fence about giving that first book a go will likely one-click-buy it at that price. Hopefully from there they get hooked into the whole series and pay full price for the subsequent books.

Bundling and staggering discounts

Similar to the above technique, another I've seen authors use is lowering the price of all the books in a series to a single discounted price point (like $0.99) for each book, and then booking paid promotion for the series as a whole.

Another option is staggering the discounts, for example:

- Book one = free
- Book two = $0.99
- Book three = $2.99
- Book four = $4.99 (full price for release)

I've seen authors share discounts like this with their own following as well as asking other authors to share to their audiences, while also booking paid promotion sites where applicable.

Boxed sets

Another completely different type of reader you might consider targeting is the boxed set reader. These readers often wait until a series is complete and bundled together in a boxed set or omnibus that they can binge.

An omnibus is usually priced at a discount compared to the individual books. So for example, *The Oremere Chronicles* books are priced like so:

- *Heart of Mist:* $4.99
- *Reign of Mist:* $4.99
- *War of Mist:* $4.99

- *Dawn of Mist:* $2.99 (This is a lower price because it's a short story collection rather than a full-length epic fantasy novel)
- Total: $17.96

The boxed set that features all four books is priced at just $9.99, offering a discount to those who want to invest in all four books at once.

How to make the most of price pulsing and discounts

Always share any sales with your newsletter and social media following – reward your fans by sharing these opportunities with them first.

As a KU author, I also always like to encourage these readers to actually purchase the book for their library when it's discounted or free, so they can reread it whenever they want and have it for their personal collection rather than just as a borrow.

Nowadays, I don't ever discount a book unless I can accompany the sale with a range of paid newsletter promotions, as explained above. This gets my book in front of a brand-new audience and stretches my reach far wider than I could otherwise achieve with just my regular following.

Sometimes it's also worth joining together with other authors in your genre for a joint sale. I've seen these used to great success across social media. Before booking your next promotion, you could always ask the authors you know if anyone else wants to do a free or $0.99 promotion. That way, you can join forces when spreading the word on social media. For example, instead of one free book, readers can be made aware of five free books via a series of Instagram posts and stories from each of the authors involved. It's completely up to you how you do it, but joining forces like this leverages everyone's audiences for maximum exposure.

SIXTEEN

In-Person Launch Events

"Come and celebrate the release of the highly anticipated fantasy debut, Heart of Mist *from local author, Helen Scheuerer. Be a part of the official launch of* Heart of Mist *at Better Read Than Dead. Free event. Drinks and nibbles. Books available to purchase on the night."*
—*Heart of Mist* Facebook event page, hosted by Helen Scheuerer & Better Read Than Dead

I DEBATED whether or not to include this chapter at all, for the simple reason that I'm no longer doing in-person events for book launches. However, they certainly played a big part in my launches during the earlier years of my career and I know some authors still love to do them, so I'll share my experiences here and you can decide if this is something you want to incorporate into your own launches.

First off: I've done both ends of the spectrum with in-person book launches – from a 100+ person party in a bookstore to a more intimate Q&A affair with around 20 people. Both options have their place, as well as their pros and cons.

The big party

For each of the main books in *The Oremere Chronicles*, I hosted a big launch party in a popular bookstore in Sydney's inner west. The biggest of these events saw over 100 people turn up to celebrate, while the smallest was about 60 people or so. These were huge affairs and involved a lot of stress, effort and cost on my part.

I provided food and drink, including cupcakes featuring the book's cover. I bulk-ordered the stock in advance, with the bookstore taking care of sales and taking a 40% cut from the RRP. I wrote and delivered a speech. My family and I drove all the food, drink and stock to and from the bookstore (not ideal with the terrible Saturday night parking in that area), and helped to set up before and clean up after the event. My sister and a friend did photography on the night so there was plenty of promotional content to use. My friend actually created a video of the *Heart of Mist* event and I reshare it on social media every year on the book's anniversary.

For each event, I created a run sheet that I shared with the people working in the bookstore (they probably thought I was a nightmare), and I checked in with them throughout the week leading up to the event about RSVPs etc. I used Facebook and my newsletter to spread word to any local readers (as well as friends and family), and the bookstore featured the event on their social media channels and in their newsletter. I was always happy with the turnout.

For me, the event wasn't so much about book sales as it was about bookending the publishing process and acknowledging the milestone. It was also a great way to get bookish friends to come together in one place and bond over their love of the genre. *And* it was an excuse to dress up, drink cheap bubbles and celebrate with the people who had been there for me along the way.

Having an event like this also lent me an air of credibility. It was hosted in a well-known store, and after each event, my book became the bestseller in the store for that week and was featured in the window display, in the store's newsletter and on their Instagram account.

However, it wasn't all fun and games. Over the three big events I hosted, there were a few challenges as well. For one of the launches, stock went missing and the bookstore tried to tell me it was a cost I had to swallow, despite the fact that they were in charge of the sales on the night and were making a 40% commission on the RRP of each book sold. Another time, they only put one staff member on the event (for over 100 people) and the poor sales assistant was flooded with people wanting to buy books, which led to the event running overtime and the staff from the downstairs part of the store getting increasingly frustrated with us.

The most unpleasant thing to have happened at one of these launches, however, was an issue with security. In the months leading up to the event, I had been harassed by someone who hadn't been accepted into an anthology I was running. Another woman and I received several nasty, threatening messages from this person and complaints were made to the police. In the lead-up to the event, I tried to put this whole ordeal out of my mind and focus on the logistics – when to pack the car, how many books to order, how we were going to find a parking space on a Saturday evening... However, on the actual night, as I was trying to take a moment for myself on the outskirts of the room after my speech (hello, introvert), I was approached by a man I didn't know. Without being able to tell you how, I knew it was him instantly. He proceeded to interrogate me about my book, until I asked him point blank if he was the person who'd been harassing me online. Every woman reading this probably understands the pit of dread and fear that opens up when you're faced with a situation like this, even in a room of 100 people.

After my brother and a friend chased him from the event (out of the bookstore and down the street, according to my brother), the man left a nasty public comment on my author Facebook page about how I was a fraud and had failed to answer his questions about my book. Fun times.

Security was not something I thought I had to worry about at the launch event for an independently published YA fantasy novel by an unknown author. As it turned out, that was an oversight on my part. For the next event, I asked some of my brother's burly friends to take on that role, and they showed up dressed for the part, which was actually kind of hilarious.

Somewhere between the *Reign of Mist* launch and the *War of Mist* launch, I moved to a small town in New

Zealand. While I flew back to Sydney for the *War of Mist* event, I decided it would be my last one for the foreseeable future.

Despite the challenges, I loved those events and they really did act as a marker for each milestone. While they weren't quite a financially savvy investment, I believe the awareness and credibility they lent me as an author, particularly in my earlier years, was worth it in spades.

A more intimate affair

As I mentioned above, somewhere between releases, I moved to New Zealand, and for the launch of *Dawn of Mist* (my prequel short story collection for *The Oremere Chronicles*), the entire country was in lockdown.

However, my next launch was for a new series starter, *A Lair of Bones*, and a local writer friend suggested I do a smaller event to celebrate. We decided on a Q&A evening where, at a small local venue (an event space attached to a bar and hotel), she and I would do a reading and then discuss the work. It was a ticketed free event that was part of the annual writers' festival for the region.

The event was advertised on the festival's Facebook page and in a handful of local magazines. About 20–30 people showed up to hear me read from my book and then discuss its themes and inspiration. For the first time in my career as a young adult author, actual *young adults* showed up to the event. Their parents had brought them along and they sat in the front row and asked questions at the end. It felt like a bit of a breakthrough moment for me.

After the formal part of the evening, my friend set up a

portable payment system and sold books for me as I signed them. Her partner, a professional photographer, took photos throughout the event, which I still use for content on social media now.

It was a vastly different experience to the big events I'd done in the past, but it also felt more suited to the times (post-lockdowns and all). Afterwards, I received emails and messages on social media from the teenagers who attended – some saying how much they loved *A Lair of Bones* and that they couldn't wait for book two, others asking for advice on getting into publishing. It was an incredibly humbling event in that respect.

The only cost to me was bulk-buying the stock in advance, most of which I sold anyway. Because the event was at a bar, guests could buy their own drinks. It wasn't appropriate to offer food, and luckily, due to the connection with the writers' festival, the venue didn't charge us a hire fee.

It was low-cost, low-stress and low-effort on my part, and worth it for the fans I gained and the books I sold without having to pay a bookstore's commission.

What now?

My approach has certainly changed over the years. I should note that when I was doing those 100+ people events, I was only releasing a book once a year. Even with my release for *A Lair of Bones*, it was just the two fiction titles that year.

Nowadays, I'm releasing more frequently – three to four books a year – and the thought of events exhausts my inner introvert. While I miss having something to mark the occasion, the truth is that the combination of where I now live and my schedule just doesn't warrant the energy spent on in-person events.

For the launch of *Dawn of Mist* over lockdown, I did an Instagram Live, and I did the same for *A Lair of Bones* in addition to the in-person event. But for the time being, I'm sticking to my celebratory social media posts and drinking wine in my PJs from the comfort of my home.

Alternatives to in-person events

I know in-person events aren't everyone's cup of tea, and that they're not always feasible for some. So, a few alternatives are:

- Instagram/TikTok Lives
- Zoom parties
- Facebook group takeovers/parties
- Streaming online Q&As with author friends

In-person event takeaways

If you're thinking of organising an event, consider the following:

- What are your goals? To sell books? To create awareness? To celebrate with your family and friends? To network within your community?
- What is your budget?

- Will you need to bulk-buy stock beforehand? Will you take pre-orders?
- Will it be a ticketed event? Free or paid?
- What is the maximum capacity of the venue and what are the restrictions, if any?
- Is the venue wheelchair-accessible?
- Do you need security?

———

As you can see, in-person events are what you make of them and can be tailored to your needs and goals. The key is to know what these are beforehand and plan accordingly.

SEVENTEEN

Marketing Between Releases

"Books only sell with a persistent, consistent focus on marketing by the author."
—Honorée Corder, *You Must Market Your Book: Increase Your Impact, Sell More Books, and Make More Money*

IN THE WORLD of traditional publishing, authors are up against a ticking clock to make the launch of their book work. Depending on the marketing budget and push from the publisher, often it's only a matter of weeks before the buzz wears off and the book fades into obscurity. The beauty of being an independently published author, however, is that you have the freedom to push a title as much as you want, for as long as you want. You can explore the numerous ways to breathe new life back into a series throughout its entire launch span and beyond.

For me, marketing between releases is a delicate

balance between three things: keeping current readers intrigued in my series, reaching new audiences and ongoing maintenance. We're going to discuss all three elements in this chapter, so let's get to it.

Keep current readers intrigued and excited

One thing I think I've done well over the years is keep my current readers invested in my ongoing series. That dates back to when I was releasing just one title a year, and continues now as I'm releasing more frequently. Regardless of your release schedule, you want to make sure your readers stay intrigued when it comes to your series. You want them marking the launch date in their calendars, counting down on social media until the big day, even taking time off work to read.

Meg Jolly shared how she does this: "I keep in touch with [readers]! Using my weekly newsletter and social media, I keep them up to date on writing progress, a little window into my life, we chat about our mutual reading, and I send any extra content related to my previous work they might enjoy, like new character artwork. It all helps maintain those lovely relationships so that when I have a new book out, they're ready, waiting, and excited to read it."

My own approach is very similar. First, any content marketing that I was doing in the lead-up to release, I continue, albeit on a smaller scale. I'm likely in the middle of drafting the next book, but I still want to engage with my current readers, so I continue to post to TikTok/Instagram with hooks from my books, pretty flatlays, and review quotes. This is also when I repost content that I was tagged in around launch – if I've been organised, I'll have a bank of images saved up that I can schedule in advance.

Next, I have a few pieces of what I call "milestone" content that I share with my existing audience between every release. This will be on all the platforms I have: Patreon, newsletter, social media, etc. Depending on what the content is, I may even book a tour for it. Milestone content is things like…

Title reveals (for the next book in the series)

I usually do this one to two weeks after the launch of the current release, as the pre-order is already live for the next book and a portion of my readership will have already jumped ahead and seen it/pre-ordered it. However, there are always readers who miss it, so I make a mini event of revealing the next title. As I mentioned earlier, this doesn't mean the book has to have a cover (in fact, I recommend that you make that a separate reveal) or a final release date, or that it even needs to be written, but a title reveal shows you're already committed to the next book and that hopefully, it won't be too long a wait until the next release.

Cover reveals (again, for the next book in the series)

Depending on your chosen genre, a cover reveal may or may not be a huge deal, so that's for you to decide.

However, in fantasy romance and its offshoots, cover reveals create immense excitement and generate a lot of buzz about a series. I usually post teasers in the lead-up to the reveal, generic "coming soon"-style posts, countdown posts, and "torn paper"-style images that show a peek of the cover (you can create images like these easily using Book Brush or something similar).

In the lead-up to my most recent cover reveal, I posted a sign-up form to my newsletter and social media, offering for people to be part of the reveal team. To my surprise, about 50 people signed up to get involved. From there, I waited until a few weeks before the reveal, then sent them an email thanking them and including the date, the relevant title information (release date, genre, tropes, blurb, etc.), and a link to a folder of assets (the high-res cover, 3D mock-ups and a list of quotes from the book they could use in their post), thus making it as easy as possible for them to create their own content and share my book with their audience. It worked a treat and it wasn't too much additional work, as I already had all the pieces.

I also booked a cover reveal tour, once again generating a bunch of content I could then reuse/repost later when I started to ramp up promotion for the upcoming release.

Cover reveals are great in that they create excitement and generate content for the author, but also in that they get the book in front of readers. At this stage, this may not directly lead to sales, but it's valuable in its exposure and its contribution to that "seven touches to sale" mentality (the idea that a customer needs to see your brand seven times before they make a decision about purchasing).

When I do a cover reveal, this is also when I start publicly talking about the pre-order being live. It's great to capture those hot leads, as there's excitement about the cover and about having something actually available for purchase for those who love the look of it from the outset and are keen to one-click-buy.

How long before the release should you do a cover reveal? There are a few factors to consider here. For example: what is the length of your overall promotional period? If you're not sharing the cover yet, have you got other creative ways to talk about the book? Personally, I like to reveal the cover roughly two to three months before the launch, simply because without the cover, I find it difficult to create the content I need for marketing. But that's also because I'm only releasing every quarter, if that, so I need to create promotional events like title and cover reveals to pique interest throughout the long tail between each release.

Excerpts/quotes

Whether it's from the current release or the book that's next in the pipeline, readers love when you share favourite quotes from your books. If it's from the current book, they can express their love for it or share their own favourite. If it's from the next book, it's a sneak peek – a titbit that they're getting to see because they're part of your community. It's exciting! Quotes and teasers like this tend to do well on social media. For a longer excerpt like a first chapter, I generally share this with my patrons on Patreon and in my newsletter in the form of a download via

BookFunnel. At the end of the content, I always include a link to the pre-order for that book.

Fellow romantasy author Clare Sager utilises a similar strategy: "I share super sneak peeks of my WIP on my Instagram Stories, letting readers nominate a word or a page number through a sticker, then I share a related snippet."

Warm reader magnets

At some point in my career I started to make the distinction between two types of reader magnets: cold and warm. We'll talk about "cold" magnets in the section for reaching new audiences, but here, we're going to talk about warm reader magnets because they're designed for your existing audience, which is hopefully already "warmed up" for your content.

To me, warm reader magnets are designed to satisfy your existing readers – those who have already read the book or series you're currently promoting, which means they already have an understanding of the characters from that series and they know how the latest book ends. Enter: the bonus epilogue and alternate POV (point of view) scenes. These have both worked well for me in terms of garnering reader excitement and satisfaction while they wait for the next book in the series.

In the back matter of *Blood & Steel*, I offered readers a download of a bonus scene. It took the ultimate steamy scene from the book (the culmination of a super slow burn, shown from the heroine's point of view) and showed it from the hero's point of view. It wasn't a major task to create this additional content; I did it in the space of an hour or less, and let me tell you... The response to this scene has been astounding. It was created for the fans and the fans answered in kind. Countless people replied saying how excited they were to read from the hero's POV, how they loved it so much they instantly pre-ordered the next book... That's the sort of buzz you want to generate!

I did a similar thing with another recent release, *Slaying the Shadow Prince*. I offered the epilogue (a wedding and wedding night) from the heroine's POV as an easy download, while also explaining that the main couple from this standalone fantasy romance would feature in the later books in my main series, *The Legends of Thezmarr*. In short, if readers were missing the FMC and MMC from *Slaying the Shadow Prince* and wanted more of them, they needed to go back and read *Blood & Steel* to get up to speed for when that couple showed up later down the line.

Before we continue: yes, this is all very romance-heavy. But I used very similar tactics between releases for both *The Oremere Chronicles* and *Curse of the Cyren Queen*, even though neither series had much romance and both were decidedly epic fantasy for young adults.

Author Steffanie Holmes does something similar for all her series starters: "I always do a bonus scene to encourage people to join my newsletter. I don't do that with every single book, but I do for the first book in a series."

For me, the point of these warm reader magnets is to repurpose and recycle content you already have, or at least have the bare bones of. You can also offer deleted scenes (I have a whole prologue for *Blood & Steel* I decided not to include in the published book, which I intend to keep for a rainy day and share with my readers), moodboards, character profiles, maps… Anything and everything you used to help you create the book itself is an option here, as long as it doesn't spoil things for later in the series!

A serial for your newsletter

In my conversation with Krystal Shannan, she explained how she writes a serial story that she sends out in her weekly newsletter to keep readers engaged between releases. This is a spin-off from one of her main series, so features a lot of familiarity for the readers and keeps them intrigued and content while they wait for her upcoming release.

Giveaways

While I try to use giveaways sparingly, they can be a lovely way to reward existing readers. For this type of giveaway, I keep it contained to my newsletter subscribers – the people who have most likely read one or more of my books, and who allow me to grace their inbox twice a month. This might be as simple as "Reply to this email with your favourite fantasy romance rec to go in the draw to win a paperback/hardcover/ebook catalogue", or it could be a bigger affair like a KingSumo or Rafflecopter giveaway. You could even combine this with a warm reader magnet (or some other digital bonus) – for example, an "Everyone wins!" competition where participants go in the draw for the main prize, but everyone gets the magnet or download.

Reach new audiences

One thing that weirdly took me a while to wrap my head around is that while keeping your existing audience happy is important, so is finding new readers to bring into the series funnel. I do this using several methods...

Continuous outreach marketing

During the lead-up to a launch, I hit the outreach marketing pretty hard, mainly contacting TikTok influencers who review similar books to mine. However, while I may take my foot off the accelerator between releases, I'm still always doing some element of this, just on a smaller scale. My current goal is to reach out to 10–20 influencers a month, offering them a copy of my first-in-series. I try to approach a combination of accounts with high followers and accounts with smaller followings but high engagement and energy. This means that while the series is releasing, there is always new life being breathed back into that first book, and that it's continually exposed to new audiences, who will hopefully have their interest piqued and give it a shot – thus bringing them into the series funnel.

Joint author promotion

This is something that is relatively new to me, as it's taken a while (read: over five years) for me to come out of my shell in the author community. However, I'm glad I have, because joint author promotions are a great way to

a) make friends with likeminded authors and b) leverage their audiences to gain exposure to your work in the same genre. I'm talking about things like newsletter swaps (which we already covered, but can be part of your general strategy for a series, not just surrounding a launch), but also things like giveaways and joint Lives on platforms like Instagram and TikTok.

If you're lucky, another author may approach you, but if you want to take matters into your own hands, organise a joint promotion yourself. Approach similar authors in your genre with a pitch. Don't just email them out of nowhere with some vague "Let's work together" line. Be straightforward and practical: what are you offering? How will this benefit them? What will be required of them? Not everyone will reply, and that's okay. Your Also Boughts on Amazon are a great place to start looking for similar authors!

Price pulsing and discounts

I'll keep this one brief, as we've already had a whole chapter dedicated to the subject; however, I want to include it here again because it's a great way to cast the net a little wider in terms of targeting discount buyers and bringing them into the series funnel. Some readers will exclusively read discounted books, and that's absolutely fine because, as an indie author, you have the flexibility to run price promotions throughout the year and over the course of your series. If you need a refresher about how this works, jump back to the chapter on price pulsing.

· · ·

Boxed sets

Another fantastic tool at our disposal is creating boxed sets of our series. You can do this for an entire series, the first few books in the series, or even a boxed set of multiple series starters. This is a great way to a) add another product or two to your backlist, b) target readers who love to binge read boxed sets and c) relaunch your series after it's complete. I love a good boxed set (or omnibus, as I refer to them on their actual product page) because there's very little additional work. You've already written the books; you just need to format them altogether (which is incredibly simple when you've got software like Vellum) and have a cover file of all books together designed. I generally think waiting six months to a year after the final book's release is best practice so as to not cannibalise your sales.

Cold reader magnets

I talk about reader magnets fairly often, as they're a tool that's worked incredibly well for me throughout my career. I categorise them into camps: the warm reader magnet (which we've already discussed) and the cold reader magnet. The cold reader magnet is designed for anyone to read without prior knowledge of your books. It's a complete story that showcases the tone and style of your writing, introduces the reader to your world and characters, and hopefully piques their interest enough for them to purchase your series starter.

I have always used a prequel for my cold reader magnet – a short story or novella that takes characters from the main series and explores a significant moment in their life that happened prior to the first book, and also shows the reader why they have a certain trait or act in a certain way in the main series.

I cover reader magnets more extensively in *How To Write A Successful Series*, but for the purpose of this chapter: a cold reader magnet is a complete story you give away for free (via a sign-up form to your newsletter) that encourages readers to take a chance on your series starter.

Maintenance

When it comes to marketing between and after releases in a series, there's a base layer of maintenance involved that I think is worth a mention here.

Hopefully at this point you're sending regular newsletters and promoting the sign-up form for your list, slowly and organically building that list. But something you may forget as you release more and more books is to update the back matter of the previous books in your series and overall catalogue, so that readers can easily find your books and be led through your body of work.

Don't forget to ask for reviews! After your initial ARC campaign and launch, it's easy to forget to prompt readers to leave reviews. I do this on social media as well as via my newsletter. I forget often enough that I now have a reminder every few weeks in my calendar to "ask for reviews".

———

When it comes down to it, the marketing between releases in your series can be just as powerful as your launch. Maintaining excitement with your current readers while attracting a new audience to the series can also make the world of difference to your next release!

Section III: Launch Case Studies

EIGHTEEN

Series Launch Case Study: The Oremere Chronicles

"The earlier in your career you are, the more this launch feels like it represents your entire career."
—Chris Fox, *Launch to Market: Easy Marketing For Authors*

SO FAR, I've given you a bunch of different strategies, from laying the groundwork and pre-launch tactics to launch marketing and all that goes in between. At the beginning of this book, I told you I'd give you the options and that it would be up to you to figure out what works best for you and your books. However, I don't want to leave it there – I want to show you how I put all these moving pieces together for my own series launches.

Before I do, I want to note a few things. First, I want to recognise that the publishing landscape has changed drastically since I published my first series, as it will continue to do over the course of all our careers. Second, in a similar vein, things that work today may not work tomorrow, or alternatively, a brand-new social media platform may spring to life and lead the charge in book sales for a particular genre. By sharing the launch case studies of my series, I'm not telling you that the way I have done things is the best step-by-step guide to series success. Rather, I'm offering examples of how you might pull together various strategies and tweak them to suit your own goals and preferences.

So, with that said, let's dig into some launch case studies…

The Oremere Chronicles (2017-2020): paperback and ebook

Since the beginning of my indie author career, I've always taken book launches incredibly seriously. In part, I think it was my background in traditional publishing, wherein I'd explored marketing and book production at length as part of my master's, and I'd made a habit of closely studying the launches of the books I liked.

However, more than anything, from the moment I decided to indie publish, I knew that I had to treat my books as a business. Why wouldn't I give my work the best chance of success by creating the most organised, structured and well-researched launches around? Why wouldn't I treat my release like a traditional publishing house would?

That was the mindset I had when I first started planning the launch of *Heart of Mist*, the first book in my YA epic fantasy trilogy, *The Oremere Chronicles*. For context,

Heart of Mist was published in 2017, *Reign of Mist* in 2018 and *War of Mist* in 2019, with a collection of prequel stories, *Dawn of Mist*, to follow in 2020. In January of 2018, I went full time as an indie author. In hindsight (what a beautiful thing that is), *The Oremere Chronicles* was a bit of an outlier in terms of success, and in my experience, in those years it was quite a different playing field when it came to gaining visibility. However, that's not to say I didn't put in the work, because my god, did I work hard for that launch. Here's what I did…

Marketing

First off, I had a professionally produced product – editing, proofing, cover and all the rest. Was it my best work? Of course not. It was my debut book – I still can't bring myself to go back and read it – but I know that it was a solid product.

Next, I embarked on a huge outreach marketing campaign for the book, which included finding ARC reviewers, getting blog features and interviews, getting traditional media coverage and planning an in-person launch event.

About four to six months prior to the release of *Heart of Mist*, I did the arduous task of creating a master spreadsheet with hundreds of platforms and blogs that featured YA fantasy books and their authors. This could be in the form of:

- Written interviews
- Podcast interview episodes

- YouTube Q&As
- Blog post cover reveals
- Book quotes or excerpts
- Guest posts from the author on a given topic
- Pinterest-friendly graphics of setting inspiration, book quotes etc.

I did all of this myself, in and around the day job I had at the time. Thanks to my degree in publishing and my own research, I had a good idea of how a marketing campaign worked and what sort of materials might be useful both to me and to anyone I was trying to work with, so I created a media kit and a press release to accompany any pitch I sent out. I personalised every pitch and made sure that I kept in line with the publication's review requirements and/or style guide. Back then I didn't even have a domain-based email address; everything was just sent from good old-fashioned Gmail.

The Oremere Chronicles' launch was the only time I tried to get traditional media coverage. My spreadsheet had about 50 entries across Australian and international media, all of whom I contacted with a press release about the upcoming release of *Heart of Mist*. Depending on my success with different platforms, I contacted them again with each new release in the series, though if memory serves, the coverage got less and less frequent.

My big win in terms of traditional media was being featured in *Bookseller and Publisher* (now called *Books+Publishing*) – potentially a slow news week for them at the time. This was more of a win in terms of validation than in sales. As someone who had studied publishing, this was the go-to news outlet for the industry at the time, and I had people from my degree get in touch saying they'd seen *Heart of Mist* featured. Nowadays, I wouldn't worry about something like this – it casts the net too widely and targets industry people rather than readers. I'd now rather spend my time finding influencers who love the genre.

In any case, when I received a positive reply to any of my outreach efforts, I was not only grateful, but went out of my way to make things as easy as possible for them by including a package of resources like an author bio, social links, website links, purchase links, book cover and author photo, without being asked. Looking back now, my *Heart of Mist* outreach content folder has 42 files, all of which were written by me and sent to a platform to be featured, be it in a written Q&A, a guest post or some sort of spotlight feature. I also made it my mission, whenever a feature was published, to share it on my own platform and tag the relevant accounts.

In terms of my ARC campaign, I only sent digital ARCs back then and it was more than enough. I must have sent out close to 100 copies, and this was long before I knew about services like BookFunnel, so it was all emails, attachments, personalised replies, and follow-ups to each and every one.

I also had a very rudimentary "street team" back then – about 16 people in a Facebook group called the "Mist Dwellers". It consisted of a few friends and one or two "superfans". As I mentioned in my chapter on street teams, this first iteration of mine was by no means extensive or sophisticated. I didn't ask much from them – only to post the cover reveal when the book was live, and to post their reviews to Amazon.

I had been posting to Instagram, Facebook and Twitter in the lead-up to each launch – pretty much all the same things I do now: title reveal, cover reveal, teasers, pretty pictures, etc., though back then I was doing it with far less knowledge about marketable tropes and comp titles. It was far less intentional.

As you know, I also had the beginnings of a newsletter. It had under 1,000 subscribers when I first launched the series, and grew to about 2,000 subscribers by the time I was nearing the final release. I kept in touch regularly and, between releases, sent three prequel short stories about the main POV characters in the series (those stories became the foundation for the collection I published in 2020).

Throughout the year in between releases, I would also periodically discount *Heart of Mist* to $0.99 or free, and utilise paid newsletter promotions like Fussy Librarian or Freebooksy, depending on what I could get and which platform was recommended by my go-to guy, David Gaughran. This led to a semi-regular wave of new readers to the series throughout the years, though I did try to do it sparingly, because you get a lower ROI each time you do a price promotion like this and hit those promotional sites.

Production and distribution

For the launch of *Heart of Mist*, I printed paperbacks through a local printer in Sydney as well as uploading to Amazon's CreateSpace (the platform before KDP for print). I didn't have a hardcover (still don't at the time of writing this), and I planned on enrolling in KU three months after release, which is what I did. After I had enrolled *Heart of Mist*, the following books were all launched into KU from the outset.

The audiobooks didn't come until later, when I was approached by audio publishers and my agent after the success of *Heart of Mist*. I signed a series-length contract for *The Oremere Chronicles* a few months after *Heart of Mist* was released, with the first audiobook from Audible to publish in April 2018 and the next books to follow a similar pattern of publication after their ebook and paperback releases.

For *The Oremere Chronicles*, I sold paperbacks directly from my website to Australia and New Zealand, which was something I phased out after I moved to New Zealand and found it increasingly difficult, and certainly not worth the time and effort financially. Like many authors, selling direct is on my radar and something I'm hoping to dip my toes back into in future.

Aggressive pricing strategy

A marked difference between my launches for *The Oremere Chronicles* and the following series was the aggressive pricing strategy I used. I didn't utilise pre-orders back then, but opted for a "live" launch wherein I pressed the "Publish" button on KDP when I wanted the book to go live. On launch, the book was priced at just $0.99.

I don't have official records from back then (a rookie mistake), but from memory, the book was priced at $0.99

for launch week, then the following week went up to $2.99, then the week after went up to full price at $4.99.

During the $0.99 launch week, I utilised a handful of paid newsletter promotions like bknights on Fiverr, but the options weren't nearly as vast as they are now – and let's face it, I probably had no idea what I was doing in terms of how to time the push or stagger the various promotions. Also, the fact that it was a "live" launch made booking things in advance harder, as these services usually want the book link or at least the ASIN ahead of time as you schedule them.

I used this $0.99 launch strategy for each book in *The Oremere Chronicles* to great effect, with each one hitting #1 in various categories across the US, UK and Australian Amazon markets.

The staggered pricing strategy was something I had read about in my research at the time, and as an unknown author, I knew I was more likely to achieve a high ranking through a discounted live launch than a long pre-order period. The staggered discount also aimed to create that "limited time offer" buzz: the sooner a reader purchased the book, the better the discount they'd get. The $0.99 price encouraged readers to buy during launch week, which in turn contributed to some great sales rankings.

"Live" launching

My strategy was to have a "soft launch" period, where I quietly hit "Publish" and received the live link to the Amazon product page, which I could send to all the people who had agreed to cross-post reviews and/or promote the book to their audiences. This gave people time to update their reviews with the purchase link for the title, and to submit their reviews to Amazon before I did my big promotional push on the official "hard" launch day.

On official launch day, I sent out a newsletter with all the relevant links to the book, posted multiple times on social media and shared any posts about the book from other people. I replied to every comment and was sure to thank anyone and everyone for their support of me and of the book.

The purpose of the live launch was to try to get a high ranking in the Amazon store, as well as snatch up those deal hunters with the $0.99 launch price. When *Heart of Mist* officially launched on August 31st, 2017, it hit #1 in all its listed categories in several different countries. It was in the top 600 of the overall Amazon store at one point, and to this day, that book has made well over six figures on its own.

The in-person event

I'll keep this part brief, because there's a lot of detail covered in the chapter on this topic, but yes – for each main book in *The Oremere Chronicles*, I did an in-person event at a popular local bookstore. As I mention in the chapter, these weren't necessarily about driving sales but rather more of a branding and awareness exercise. They were also far more doable in a pre-COVID, one-release-a-year world. However, it's worth noting that there were advantages I can't necessarily measure – each book becoming the bestseller of the store during launch week and the social proof that gave each title, the buzz around the event itself, and the content it generated for social media (more social proof and credibility for me as an unknown author).

Driving subsequent sales

Because I was "live" launching, there were no pre-order chains to manage, and because the books were released roughly a year apart, I didn't automatically announce the title of the next book upon release of the current one. The main driving force of sales from one book to the next was my newsletter, however modest it was at the time.

At the back of the books then was a call for reviews, an author bio, and in the ebook edition, a call to action to join my mailing list for a prequel story. That was it. So, in the year between releases, it was up to me to keep my books at the forefront of my readers' minds, and I did that using the methods I outlined in the chapter on marketing between releases: sending prequel stories, and keeping readers posted on my writing and production processes. I even recorded very basic mini podcast episodes at one point, just to change things up a bit. I did title announcements and cover reveals, shared excerpts and all the rest between releases, and come release day, did the big launch email blast, the mop-up email and posts on social media.

Lessons learned

The launch of my first series spanned the course of

four years and there were many lessons to be learned along the way. Here are the takeaways…

- Reuse and repurpose effective content. You don't have to post brand-new content all the time. Nearly six years later, I'm still tweaking and recycling newsletters and social media posts from those earlier launches
- If something works, note it down. Create a blueprint of what works throughout your launches and use the same strategies again! The general skeleton of my launch strategies hasn't changed in all this time, because I found something that works and recreate it with each release
- Figure out your limitations/boiling point. For me, that was the in-person events. By the third launch party for *War of Mist* in 2019, I was done. I'm an introvert at heart, and talking to 100+ people at an event, making a speech and all that jazz really took it out of me, not to mention all the stress and prep in the lead-up
- Scheduling is my friend. Again, this will depend on your personality type, but being the control freak and future-orientated person that I am, I prefer to plan things in advance and be able to set and forget. That's one of several reasons that I no longer go with live launches
- It's never going to be perfect. One particular example of this is ordering six proof copy rounds of *Heart of Mist* and getting increasingly

frustrated when I kept finding very minor "errors". This was so time-consuming, costly and defeating. Since then, I've got more sets of eyes on the proof pages before they go to the printer, and once they've been to print, I limit myself to two proof copies at most

- A collection of stories is not the same as a full-length book. Ahh, this was one of the hardest lessons I learned with the releases of *The Oremere Chronicles*. I released *Dawn of Mist* in April 2020 – not a great time in the broader sense of the world being on fire etc., but more than that, my expectations were completely out of whack. I thought this 300+ page book of short stories would garner the same response and income that my 500+ page epic fantasy novels did. I was wrong

NINETEEN

Series Launch Case Study: Curse of the Cyren Queen

"Launches always bring out this odd, reflective melancholy for me. I suppose it's that everything you've worked for, for however long, comes to a head and then the next looming mountain of a task awaits."
(Author Diaries, February 9th, 2023)

BEFORE WE DEEP dive into how I put all the puzzle pieces together to launch *Curse of the Cyren Queen* in 2021, I want to set the scene for you. From the launch of *Heart of Mist* in 2017 to the launch of *Dawn of Mist* in 2020, *The Oremere Chronicles* as a series had earned well over a quarter of a million dollars, but three years after the first book came out, I slowly started to see a decline in sales. I thought that the publication of *Dawn of Mist* and the omnibus of the series in October that year would see me through until my next full-length release in 2021. That was a naive assumption on my part and saw the first financial "dip" of my career.

However, the success of *The Oremere Chronicles* spurred me on to write and publish my next young adult fantasy series, *Curse of the Cyren Queen*, and that's the series we'll take a look at now.

Curse of the Cyren Queen (2021-2022): paperback, hardcover and ebook

In my mind, *Curse of the Cyren Queen* was bigger and better than the *Oremere* books in every respect. I had written it with the market in mind, with tropes and comp titles prepared in advance; I had studied the popular covers in the genre; *and* I had stockpiled the first two books in the series, with a view to publish two per year, doubling my output. Not to mention, I'd improved as a writer (or so I hope). Overall, the structure and craft of the *Cyren Queen* books was better than my first series.

For context, book one, *A Lair of Bones*, was published in July 2021, with book two, *With Dagger and Song*, released in November of the same year. Book three, *The Fabric of Chaos*, followed in April 2022, and the fourth and final book, *To Wield a Crown*, concluded the series in September 2022.

So let's take a look at the series launch…

Marketing

I started out with much the same marketing strategy for *A Lair of Bones* as I had for the launches of the books in

The Oremere Chronicles. I even used the same spreadsheet for the bloggers I'd worked with. However, I was disappointed to discover that many of the blogs I had worked with during my first series were no longer live. Many of the URLs now redirected to a 404 error page, or a post that detailed why the blogger had retired from posting. This put a bit of a spanner in the works for me, as I had fully intended to use the same outreach marketing campaign for this new series.

I contacted those who were still posting and reviewing books, but realised quite quickly that if I wanted the same sort of reach as I'd had for *The Oremere Chronicles,* I'd have to push beyond the platforms I'd used then.

In addition to the baseline of reviewers and bloggers I'd worked with for *Oremere,* I also booked several Instagram tours (TikTok hadn't quite exploded at the time). This involved sending copies to some of the larger influencers, which was something I hadn't done before. The results were mixed in terms of the quality of the posts, and for the *ALOB* launch in particular, I'm not sure the cost of the tours and the physical copies was worth it in the end.

I wrote three prequel novellas and sent them to my existing newsletter to get them excited for the new series, while also marketing these prequel stories as cold reader magnets via social media. I also went a step further this time and had them professionally covered to match the series (something I hadn't done with any of the *Oremere* magnets).

Funnily enough, beyond my ARC campaign, I actually forgot all about having a street team for this series.

Arguably, I had a skeleton crew who helped share covers on Instagram and posted early reviews, but I didn't utilise that tiny Facebook group called the "Mist Dwellers", and I certainly didn't have the organised team I have now for my current series.

I did all the usual content marketing I'd done for *Oremere*: title reveal, cover reveal, teasers, pretty pictures, etc., but with more frequency. I also decided that there was little point to me posting on Twitter, so I cut that platform from my roster.

Towards the later releases in the series, TikTok started to gain a lot of publicity and momentum, so I did a few posts there – but in doing so I realised that I hadn't done as much upfront market research as I'd thought. I didn't have as many hooks readily available, nor tropes or "pull quotes", as I've come to call them. This is coming from someone who really thought they'd nailed their market research at the beginning of the series; it turned out to be a much bigger beast than I realised, even on my second series. But we'll get to that in the next case study.

I became far more strategic with my newsletters – sending them twice a month, as well as now experimenting with newsletter swaps. In hindsight, I cast the net too wide here, and have since reined things back in to only include very close comp titles and authors in the same subgenre.

I also got more serious about newsletter building at this stage. I had my cold reader magnets with professional covers, and I experimented with Facebook ads for them before giving up – because frankly, it was just another thing I had to manage and I didn't have the bandwidth.

I did a few promotions via BookFunnel and

BookSweeps, gaining a couple hundred subscribers to add to my list each time. I also discovered larger builders, which I invested in twice over the course of this series, adding 2,000+ subscribers to my list.

Since my initial *Oremere* days of under 1,000 subscribers, I had slowly built my list both organically and with the help of builders to somewhere in the region of 5,000 to 6,000 subscribers. I emailed them all the usual content between releases, the same as I had done for *Oremere*, with a little more frequency now, as well as any price promotions for all my books throughout the year (more on that in a moment).

Production and distribution

For *A Lair of Bones* and the subsequent launches in the series, I released the book in ebook, KU (from the start), paperback via Ingram and KDP, and hardcover via Ingram. Because of the success of *The Oremere Chronicles*, my agent was able to pitch the *Curse of the Cyren Queen* series to audiobook publishers, and we signed a series deal with Podium. As such, the audiobook for *A Lair of Bones* released shortly after the other editions, which was as close to a simultaneous release as I've gotten so far.

It was around this time that I stopped selling print books directly via my website, and at the time it was no major loss. Instead it freed up a bit of mental space and was one less thing I had to worry about. Again, selling direct is something I'm still very much interested in, particularly now there are so many wonderful options available. It's on the cards for the future!

. . .

Pricing strategy

Here's where things start to look quite different to my previous launches. It had been nearly four years since the release of *Heart of Mist* and I made the decision that I no longer wanted to launch at $0.99, nor did I want to "live" launch. Truth be told, life had been difficult for a myriad of reasons in that year between full-length releases, and I needed to be able to plan and schedule to help keep me on track. So I set up a pre-order for *A Lair of Bones* at full price ($4.99 USD). With the link handy, I was able to coordinate with other authors for newsletter swaps, send reviewers the link to include in their posts, and schedule my newsletter and all the rest in advance – a heavy weight off my shoulders.

Curse of the Cyren Queen was also the series in which I started utilising the pre-order chaining method. So when *A Lair of Bones* launched in July 2021, the link to the pre-order for *With Dagger and Song* was at the back waiting for keen readers. It worked incredibly well, and I found that with each new pre-order that went live, by launch day it always had significantly more units moved than the last book. This is a great representation of the high read-through rate the series had, particularly as it was enrolled in KU.

Being able to utilise pre-orders made each launch a lot less stressful for me. I wasn't always waiting until the last minute to receive the link and do a million tasks. Now, I could get the link and work through my list at a steady pace.

Curse of the Cyren Queen was also the series wherein I became a lot more intentional about my pricing strategies over the course of the series launches. With *Oremere*, I did $0.99 and free sales throughout the year, but this wasn't as strategic as the decisions I made with *Curse of the Cyren Queen*. Again, I modelled these price pulses and discounts off David Gaughran's model.

A Lair of Bones launched at $4.99, so that when book two (*With Dagger and Song*) launched four months later, I could discount book one to $0.99 and arrange a bunch of paid newsletter promotion slots to reach new readers. These were staggered over the course of a week to encourage a long tail of sales rather than a single spike.

When book three launched, I did the same again, and when book four launched, I went big and made *A Lair of Bones* free for a week. Throughout that week, I staggered paid newsletter promotions across multiple days, again aiming for the long tail of sales, not a huge one-off spike. I also posted about it on my own social media and sent the sale to my newsletter list, always saying something along the lines of "To celebrate the release of [Title], I've discounted book one to [price]". It was a great way to get those readers who'd been sitting on the fence about trying the book to take the plunge. It also leveraged the exposure of the new book to convince new readers to give the series a go, especially once it was complete and ready to binge.

Pre-order strategy

This series was the first time I had utilised pre-orders, so I created incentives (as discussed in the earlier chapter on pre-orders). This took a lot of the urgency and stress of the launch away for me, and I found that creating pre-order chains was incredibly effective in terms of both sales and creating early excitement for the next book in the series.

Events

So, here is where I deviated from my first series launch blueprint again… As I mentioned in the chapter on in-person events, I did end up doing a smaller event for *A Lair of Bones*: an intimate Q&A gathering at a local venue. This was much more my speed and it involved *significantly* less stress and work on my part. I just had to bring the books and show up to answer questions.

For *A Lair of Bones* I also did a live Instagram Q&A, which was a very casual affair that involved me sitting in front of the camera, drinking a cocktail and answering questions that people had sent in over the previous week.

After those two lovely smaller events, I was releasing more frequently than I had been in the past. The next book in the series launched just four months later, and the next one just five months after that (which was fast for me). Ultimately, I decided that for the time being, in-person events and even those on Instagram Live just weren't my cup of tea. It's something I might revisit in the future, but for now, I'm happy with a nice bottle of wine and my partner for company at home, toasting to the book. I realised my time and mental energy were better spent elsewhere in my business.

. . .

Lessons learned

The series launches for *Oremere* and *Cyren Queen* were vastly different in terms of style, frequency and financial outcomes. Both series were successful by my definitions, but the learning curve between the two was significant. Here are the takeaways:

- Manage your expectations. I had no idea how wrong I could be in terms of my expectations of sales for both series. The runaway success of one series does not define the success of the next, nor does suddenly increasing your production rate. I doubled the number of books I published per year, but it didn't double my income
- When you think you've done enough market research, think again
- Find what works for you and iterate it. When something changes, find a new tactic to try. Always be building your arsenal of tools for launches, because that's the thing – the industry is constantly changing and you have to be able to pivot with it
- Cut the things that don't make you feel good. Always

TWENTY

Current Series Launch Strategy

"Well, it's all over again, another book launch done and dusted. It's a weird feeling really – all that work for one day of hype. But of course, it's not really about launch day at the end of it all, it's about adding to my catalogue and slowly increasing my readership and sales. Despite all the fuss about rankings on release, it's actually about the long game."
(Author Diaries, April 18th, 2020)

THROUGHOUT THE FIRST five years of my full-time indie career publishing series, my general approach to launch strategies has been one of iteration, tweaking and refining. For the most part, with each launch I try something new and assess its contribution to the success of the series or that particular launch within it.

It's been an interesting process, to say the least, particularly as each series has been different in its market and genre. Sure, my first two series were both young adult epic fantasy, but they were different in so many ways: different points of view (multiple vs. single), trilogy vs. quartet, different pricing, different release schedules… and that's all just the tip of the iceberg. I certainly learned a lot along the way about writing more to market (which makes launching and marketing so much easier), and I learned a lot about my own abilities and limitations.

Particularly as I release more books annually compared to my original one per year, I've found that I need to preserve energy in my approach to launches. If I want to write and produce four books a year, as well as publish four books a year, I can't have four massive launches. It leaves little room for anything else. What about holidays? Bouts of sickness? Mental health? I'm in this career for the long haul, which means it has to be sustainable and that I need to give each series every possible chance at success.

Which brings us to my current series launch strategy…

The Legends of Thezmarr (2023-2024): ebook, paperback, hardcover

Amidst launching my two previous series, I delved deep into the craft and market research of bestselling books. I read books like *Romancing the Beat* by Gwen Hayes, *Romance Your Brand* by Zoe York and pretty much all of Elana Johnson's nonfiction offerings. (It's no surprise that I quote all of these books in *How To Write A Successful Series*, because they showed me that the success of a book starts long before you release it into the world.) T. Taylor's *7 Figure Fiction* was another eye-opening read for me. Essentially, what I learned in reading these titles was that while I *thought* I had done market research for *Oremere* and *Cyren Queen*, I had barely scratched the surface.

When it came to my next series, *The Legends of Thezmarr*, I was determined to dive deeper. I had already decided throughout the release of the *Curse of the Cyren Queen* series that it was time I moved into a romance subgenre. I was reading and enjoying more adult romance titles than I ever had before, and a common theme throughout the reviews of my previous books was a desire to see more romance.

So with the decision to move into the adult romantic fantasy space made, I started my research. I devoured and deconstructed books in this genre. I talked to other authors who were doing well in this area and asked them about the nuances between romantic fantasy and fantasy romance – terms that readers often use interchangeably, but that actually have slight differences. I ran my rough ideas for this new series past two successful authors in the genre who were generous enough to chat with me and offer their insights.

I read the K-lytics report on fantasy romance, and did the same again when it came out again the following year. I studied romance craft books, books on writing to market – just about anything I could get my hands on. Jennifer Lynn Barnes' talk on "Writing for Your Id" for Romance Writers of America was another great, informative resource. I joined Facebook groups where readers discussed their favourite books in the genre; I read reviews of bestselling titles and noted the things readers liked and didn't like; I noted down popular tropes and character archetypes; I studied what successful authors were doing in terms of the types of editions they offered.

For every resource and task mentioned here, I promise there were a dozen more. It was a huge undertaking, but worth it in so many ways. What I learned was that the success of an entire series is baked into the books themselves, and so all of this work was necessary before I put pen to paper and ultimately launched the series. This upfront work was one of the key differences between my previous series launches and the launches I do now.

Okay, now I've stressed that point so thoroughly, what else did I do?

Production and distribution

From my extensive research, I knew a few things about the expectations of readers in my particular genre: most of the bestselling titles were in KU, most were upwards of 500 pages, and the editions offered were a paperback as well as a pretty hardcover with a different case design under the dust jacket. So I set out to meet these expectations.

I launched *Blood & Steel*, book one in *The Legends of Thezmarr*, in February 2023 with ebook (in KU), paperback (KDP and Ingram) and hardcover (Ingram) editions. A mere six weeks after release, it became my most successful launch since 2019.

Interestingly, the print copies have exceeded all my expectations despite their high price point (they're big books), and the visibility for the series has been incredible so far. *Blood & Steel* has also garnered more reviews in a shorter space of time than any of my other books. At six weeks old, it had more reviews than *A Lair of Bones* had after nearly two years.

Marketing

The first thing I decided when it came to marketing the launch of this new series was that a huge outreach marketing campaign to book bloggers was no longer effective. My list of over a hundred websites had dwindled down to only a few that were still active, so I figured it just wasn't worth my time and energy going down that road again. Instead, I turned to what my fellow authors were doing to see what might work for me.

TikTok and Instagram were the noteworthy platforms creating buzz about books in my subgenre, so I started there. I created a list of accounts who seemed to love the comp titles for my books, I drafted outreach emails to them, and when the time came, I bit the bullet and emailed them with a pitch for *Blood & Steel* that included my trusty media kit with all the information about the book. I told myself that where I'd saved money on elements of production, I could invest in sending more copies to influencers. At the start, I decided I'd only do paperbacks because they were cheaper, but as I slowly saw more and more reactions to the hardcover, I figured that was actually a better investment – my audience loves a beautiful hardcover.

In addition to my own outreach marketing, I booked several Instagram and TikTok tours with various services. I did this for the cover reveal, an ARC campaign and a general release blast. As I mentioned before, it's hard to determine a measure of success for investments like this, but as I started to see the book being discussed outside of my initial circle, I decided it had been worth it. Not to mention that the content these creators were producing was beautiful and something that I could repost not only throughout the launch period, but throughout the series' entire lifespan. I staggered these tours similarly to how I'd stagger a paid newsletter promotion campaign – over the course of several days or even weeks, so there was a steady stream of new content and new people posting about the book for a prolonged period of time, rather than a huge spike and then crickets.

My ARC campaign was another beast. I wanted to go hard here and get the book into as many hands as possible. I approached my regular team, as well as posting in a few ARC Facebook groups for fantasy romance/romantic fantasy readers. For previous launches I'd sent between 30–50 ARCs each time, whereas for this new series launch, I sent well over 100 digital copies out to reviewers, plus print editions.

The launch of this series was also the first time I utilised an official street team since the 16 "Mist Dwellers" back in 2017. I opened a Discord server, The Laughing Fox, and the people who participated were worth their weight in gold. As I mentioned in the chapter on this topic, it was a lot of work, but now I have the blueprint for every street team in future. For a refresher of how I managed it, head back to Chapter 9.

My newsletter marketing was much the same as it had always been in terms of content: cover reveal, excerpts, early reviews, countdowns and pretty pictures. I did, however, dip my toes back into swapping with other authors. This time around, I was far more selective about the authors I chose to work with. Either I had read their books myself (as part of my research), I knew them personally, or their books were all the rage and highly rated, as well as having a similar cover design to my own. Again, I approached these swaps at a slow and steady pace, similar to staggering the tours. I wanted a steady drip of promotion over the course of the book's release and afterwards as well.

My social media strategy also remained largely unchanged, with the exception of adding TikTok to the mix. (I can hear the groans from the indie author community from my office in New Zealand.) The thing is, I'm not overly great at TikTok and I don't have a lot of followers, but it does help. Even when my videos only get 200 views, it's 200 views I wouldn't have got otherwise, and they're worth something to me. I had played with the platform for the launch of *To Wield a Crown* and then promptly dropped it, as it felt like too much work. But with *Blood & Steel*, because all that marketing was baked into the book itself, it was so much easier to come up with text for videos – quotes from the book, hooks, tropes, etc. And then I could strip the TikTok logo from the videos and repost everything to Instagram as Reels, so repurposing the content has been a dream.

Another key point of difference between the launch of this series and the previous ones is that I haven't stopped that initial TikTok/influencer outreach. Part of my strategy is to continue to put *Blood & Steel* into the hands of new readers over the course of the series, so I'm constantly finding new audiences for it.

Paid advertising

I've said it before and I'll say it again: I'm no ads expert. But when it came to *Blood & Steel*, I was excited about what sort of ROI I could get from ads on a book that was actually written and designed to market. I set up a bunch of ads on Amazon, which is my only advertising platform currently (with a view to experimenting with Facebook at some stage), but I've found that the majority of them aren't moving the dial much. This was why I made the decision to do the bare minimum on AMS ads and invest the extra money I would have spent there on sending out copies to influencers instead.

Of course, that may change somewhere down the line, but the main takeaway I have from this decision is that I'd much rather spend my time connecting with actual readers than pulling my hair out over bids and getting my cost per click down.

It's also a matter of it being early in the life of the series. I've made a note in my calendar to reassess things when the series is further along and I have a little more wriggle room in terms of a higher profit margin on the overall series.

Pricing and pre-order strategy

After doing my research, I found that most books in my genre were still being priced at $4.99 USD, so I stuck with that as my price point, in addition to being enrolled in KU. Linking my pre-orders had worked well for my previous series, and it was also the strategy I saw a lot of similar authors adopting in my genre, so I maintained that approach as well. So far, it's worked incredibly well.

For the initial pre-order for *Blood & Steel*, I offered a pre-order incentive to those who submitted their proof of purchase to a designated email address. Those who forwarded this to me received:

- The first 30 pages of the book
- A downloadable map
- The Spotify playlist I used while writing the book
- A visual guide I created for the world

This definitely incentivised people to pre-order, and I received a lot of excitement to that particular email address about the upcoming release, which was really lovely to see in the lead-up to launching into a new subgenre.

Driving subsequent sales

In addition to the pre-order chain, which naturally drives sales to the subsequent books in the series, I'm using a combination of continuous outreach marketing to influencers, as well as content marketing to social media and my newsletter.

· · ·

Lessons learned

As I said to a coaching client the other day, the learning in this industry is endless, so naturally with another series launch came more lessons learned...

- The power of writing to market was abundantly clear in this launch case study. The buzz about the book's tropes was almost palpable and I could see it gaining traction in real time
- While I'm not a TikTok expert, connecting with likeminded readers and influencers has been incredible, and I've been able to leverage other people's platforms to gain exposure for the series starter
- While the book didn't gain any bestseller tags upon launch, at six weeks old it had already outsold more than half the books in my current catalogue at the time of writing this

TWENTY-ONE

Launch Snapshot

"Well, it's certainly been a strange launch day. One minute I'm at ease with the fact that this launch is different because of circumstances beyond my control, and the next minute I'm quite defeated that this book came together over the course of four years and this is how it's brought into the world... Quietly. Very quietly."
(Author Diaries, April 16th, 2020)

SO FAR, I've done my best to provide you with an in-depth look at the strategies I've used over the course of my series launches. However, if you're anything like me, you might want to look at some of the details on a more granular level. If not, feel free to skip ahead, but I thought it might be useful to show a breakdown of the kinds of tasks I do on the launch week and launch day for each book in my series.

As you've probably gathered, each launch is unique in

its own way, and a launch will look different for everyone. One thing in particular to note in my case is that a launch day for me spans across two days because of the time difference between New Zealand (previously Australia) and the rest of the world. When it's technically launch day for me, I'm generally waiting until the US and UK (my biggest markets) wake up and get their notifications. Just quietly, I hate this aspect, as it feels like I'm lagging behind time, but it's just what launches are like when you live on this side of the world.

Anyway, it's strange seeing these tasks all written out, because in the context of this book, it doesn't actually seem like much – but that's because so much of the work is done in the lead-up to release. Just keep that in mind!

So, here's a snapshot of the tasks I do both on launch week and on launch day…

Launch week

- Last minute check that all information and files in KDP are correct
- Double-check everything has been scheduled correctly (social media, newsletters etc.)
- Update website links page to "Available now"
- Update back matter of previous book to say "Available now"
- Check in with any tour services
- Submit print files to KDP
- Check ebook, paperback and hardcover editions are linked on the Amazon product

page
- Batch launch TikToks if not already done
- Sort previous week's prize for street team
- Write and schedule pre-order incentive thank you message
- Post 2 x daily TikToks
- Engage with/reply to comments, posts, shares on socials to drum up excitement
- Review launch day list

Launch day

- Check delivered Kindle files
- Check in with street team manager
- Send street team personal message/thanks
- Post AM TikTok (save and schedule as a Reel for following day)
- Post PM TikTok (save and schedule as a Reel for following day)
- Check rankings (prematurely of course)
- Pin social posts to top of profile
- Update social media headers
- Repost and engage on socials
- Save Instagram images for later use and thank those who posted
- Claim book on BookBub (ensure I'm listed as the author – this prompts BookBub to send a New Release alert to anyone following me)
- Try to work a regular(ish) day but be forgiving of distractions

. . .

Without the fanfare/stress of an in-person event, and the more I release, the more this becomes just part of my job. There's a surreal apathy to it, at least for me and the authors I've talked to (I'll touch on self-care later) – but for the most part, because I've had the pre-order link in advance, I've been able to schedule the majority of my promotion in advance, and now it's just a matter of keeping an eye on things as they unfold. Does it sound a little anticlimactic? Let me share some of my thoughts on that...

> *"Another launch day arrives and with it comes an anticlimax. I wonder if this is how it is once your passion becomes your career? It's just like any other day really. There is no big celebration, no moment of realisation that you've put another book out in the world. No tearful moment of joy...*
>
> *I actually think all that comes in the quieter moments. Like the afternoon you place that new author copy on your shelf alongside all the others. Or the moment you sign off the final cover, or receive that first bit of feedback.*
>
> *Launch day becomes something else when you're seven books in, when you're releasing more than once per year. It's a lonely day, punctuated by the excitement of others, which you in turn are pressured to mirror but don't actually feel yourself.*
>
> *Now, it's not a matter of what this book means to you, but rather, what project comes next and how fast can you get there.*
>
> *Today, I feel the weight of the series that comes next, which is still two books away from now." (Author Diaries, April 21st, 2022)*

Section IV: All the Rest

TWENTY-TWO

Self-Care for Series Launching

"I don't feel anything about the upcoming launch but detachment. Is this the way it will be from now on? The more books you publish and the more frequently you do so, the less you care? Or is it because it's a middle book in a series and I haven't planned as much fanfare as I would for a first or last in a series?"
(Author Diaries, April 5th, 2022)

IF YOU WANT to sustain an indie author career long term, there's no getting around the fact that you need to take care of yourself. Self-care and creating a sustainable business model are by no means new topics in our industry, but they're discussed time and time again because of a) how important they are and b) how common it is for authors to push them to the side.

Many aspects of this career can be stressful, and I know I'm not the only one who has felt the burn of the hustle and the pressure to hit targets and goals. I've had countless conversations with my author friends about burnout, about the lies we tell ourselves in order to keep working when we need rest, and about the financial pressures of the job... It could be a book in itself. (Actually, if this is resonating deeply with you, check out Becca Syme's book, *Dear Writer, Are You In Burnout?*.)

As I was outlining and researching for this book, the topic of self-care came up numerous times, and as someone who is guilty of letting this aspect of author life slide, I felt it was important to dedicate a chapter to it. But before we dive in, I'll get the usual spiel out of the way: I'm not a mental health care professional. Everything I'm about to cover is either based on personal experience or the conversations I've had with other successful series authors, so please bear that in mind.

On my side of things, I'm a bit of a stress-head in general. I worry constantly, over big things, little things and everything in between. It's something I'm slowly trying to work on, but it's ingrained deeply – combine that with a career path that can be unpredictable, and it can lead to one very tightly wound author. Often, this career is full of stress and unknowns, and each launch is rife with these things. The things I stress about around launch time (and a lot of other times, too) are: reviews, rankings, earning back my investment, deadlines, chasing people to do what I've hired them to do, finishing one thing only to remember the next project is always waiting... And of course, there's the knowledge that I could always be doing more. So, how do I cope with all this while launching my books?

Manage expectations

This is a relatively new tactic of mine and one that I'm still trying to master, but managing expectations is key to both avoiding devastation and giving yourself context for the results you're seeing. After the success of *The Oremere Chronicles*, I didn't manage my expectations for the launch of *Curse of the Cyren Queen* very well at all. I made the rookie mistake of thinking that my second series would do just as well – that the sales of the first series predicted the sales of the second.

We all make mistakes, right? This was one of mine. The thing is, *Curse of the Cyren Queen* still did well; it was still a "success" by my own measures, but those dashed expectations? They hit me hard and threw into question everything that I was doing.

I've talked about this a few times before, but essentially, I didn't take into consideration the array of factors that had changed – which, again, was a newbie error. There was the content of the series itself, but there were also external factors: pricing strategy, launching after the "gold rush" years, launching in a post-COVID world, the change in platforms used to market... There was also the fact that I hadn't published a full-length novel for about two years. Though I had only been publishing once per year prior to that, the gap in my publication schedule was significant. I thought I'd be launching to the warm audience of *The Oremere Chronicles*, but for the most part, it had been so long since I'd released a book that a lot of that audience didn't follow me across to *Curse of the Cyren Queen*, even though there was a direct link between the two series and they were in the same genre.

When it came to launching *The Legends of Thezmarr* series, I knew I had to do things differently in order to manage my expectations effectively. Ultimately, though, it involved setting a range of goals: lowball (for if things went badly), mid-level (if things went okay) and high-level (if things went really well). These goals were not set using the numbers of my most successful launches, but of my worst. I knew that if I didn't hit those goals, something was very wrong, and something needed to change.

Clare Sager has a similar approach: "I tend to set good/better/best goals, which does help, especially if the good goal is easily achievable. Having a mix of qualitative and quantitative goals helps too – those immeasurable moments when a reader emails you about your book are just as important as ranks or sales!"

Meg Jolly also shared how she manages her expectations around a launch:

"My focus is usually on what's within my control. Do I want a million downloads and my book taking over BookTok? Well, wouldn't that be nice! Do I plan for that or expect it? Absolutely not. I always look at what the cold, hard reality is of what I can personally be certain of delivering. For me, it's making sure I am meeting my reader's expectations and giving them a fantastic reading experience – that's my #1. My #2 is usually the practical aspect of making sure all my pre-order files are uploaded and ready to go so I know that there'll be no hiccups – my readers get their book, and I get my pre-orders. Because I normally do pre-orders on sequels, that's a really good way for me to keep my

expectations in line with reality. To keep pushing for the very best pre-order run I can get, without getting my head lost in the clouds of wishful thinking that's later disappointed!

Ultimately, I have to manage those expectations from a standpoint of: what do I want? What is achievable? What would be comfortable? What would be a reasonable stretch? And, am I building a launch experience that energises me rather than drains me?"

From this you can probably see that managing my own expectations also involved talking to other authors about what to expect in terms of pre-orders when I was in KU, as well as acknowledging that while I had more than five years of publishing under my belt, I was moving into a new subgenre where I didn't have an existing audience.

Having people I could talk to about these things helped significantly. When I launched *The Oremere Chronicles*, I didn't have many indie author friends to talk to, and when I launched *Curse of the Cyren Queen*, I was only just starting to forge the friendships I have today with other indie authors who I now lean on heavily for support and knowledge. Which leads nicely into…

Find your people

I've talked a bit about this on podcasts and in my newsletter, but I cannot stress enough how important it is to make friends with other authors. You can have the most supportive family in the world, but they'll never completely understand the nuances of what you do, nor will they have the answers when things go wrong. And things *will* go wrong (we'll get to that in a moment).

Every time I have faced some sort of author hurdle in the last few years, it's been my indie author friends who have kept my sanity in check, who have helped me come up with solutions, who have listened to me freak out with a sympathetic ear. These are the people who will tell you to slow down when you're taking too much on; they're the people who'll tell you that it's okay to read a book instead of write, because you need the inspiration. They're the people who will sit with you while you muddle your way through a production calendar and plan your launches for the year.

Reaching out and meeting new people doesn't come naturally to me, and it took me a long time to find the people I connect with the most, but now? Now, those people are the authors who look out for me when I'm not looking out for myself.

I reflected a little on this in my author diaries:

"A change in subgenre and a lot of new ventures on my plate have left the tank a little empty when it comes to planning the next launch.

I spoke to C yesterday and we compared launch plans. I think there's a part of me (the strategic part apparently) that's always seeking a silver bullet, always wondering if I'm missing something critical in terms of my plans and making them better.

The exercise yesterday showed me that it's not the case at all. Most of us are doing the same things and it's a bit random how well you do to a certain extent. Obviously you have to write the *best book you can, but..." (Author Diaries, October 18th, 2022)*

The crash-and-burn of launching

In scouring my journals for inspiration for this book, I came across the delightful self-posed question: *"Should I take a break before I break down?"*. I had to laugh.

When it comes to launch time, I operate at 110% before I crash and burn. I think an element of this is all the interactions with people I don't normally speak to; a state of being "on" all the time. There's a nagging sense of stress that comes with not wanting to miss an opportunity or a window to promote your book.

When I launched *Heart of Mist* in 2017 (while working a day job), I crashed and burned *hard*. After that week, I could have slept for a year. I was exhausted and bone-weary, and truth be told, I stupidly wore that like a badge of honour (that cult of busyness is still something I'm trying to unlearn). I thought being that tired was part of being an author around launch time, that it made me more of a "real" author.

As I published more frequently, I realised I couldn't afford to crash and burn regularly like that, and I was sick of being tired. So, while there's still always *some* element of this exhaustion (again, for me I think it's the social side of things), I've learned to streamline my launch processes over the years to avoid the worst of it. So, what have I done to achieve some semblance of order amidst the series launch chaos?

First, batching and scheduling content is a lifesaver for

me. As I mentioned, I have templates saved and I reuse content and captions all the time. I use the same launch templates for newsletters with minor adjustments, I use the same outreach email template, I have a bank of generic social media questions… Having a go-to pool of content like this eliminates so much decision fatigue for me. I'm not having to sit here with a million other things on my mind, trying to come up with a caption for a photo.

I also try to keep things sustainable in the regularity with which I post. For example, during my most recent release, I posted to social media daily, sometimes even twice a day; however, during the "downtime" between releases/when I'm not in "hype mode", I cut back to three times a week, and if I miss something, I do my utmost to be kind to myself. I doubt anyone is glued to their phone wondering why I haven't posted to Instagram at 11am on a Tuesday.

I also try to remove the urgency and the immediacy of everything. Believe me, I've fallen into the throes of this pressure on numerous occasions, and I still do every now and then: "It doesn't seem to matter that I do this full time, I never seem to have enough hours in the day, or more than that, the drive to try every single little thing in the hopes that it moves the dial in a way that makes the effort worth it." (Author Diaries, April 5th, 2022)

However, indie publishing is all about the long game, and shifting my mindset has helped rein in any panic attacks over rankings, the speed of reviews coming in etc. I even apply it to things like responding to emails. I've stopped trying to do *everything*.

When I chatted to Steffanie Holmes, she highlighted

the importance of avoiding burnout at all costs: "In my last year of working for 'the man' I had burnout… A very big part of my writing business is about never ever going to that place again… If I start to feel that things are getting too much, I just drop stuff. I will make a list of everything that has to be done for a launch and I just look for the stuff that has the biggest bang for my time. And that stuff I will do and I will drop anything below that line."

I related hard to what Steff said, and I'm still working on trying to calm that voice that tells me I must do everything. As of writing this book, my advertising is on the backburner, as are my plans to sell direct. I'm also quelling the urge to run a Kickstarter and create special anniversary editions of *The Oremere Chronicles*. My mind tends to tell me lies about how much time has passed, pushing me onto the next thing before the dust has even settled after the last big project. Instead, I try to check in with myself – for example: has it really been three months? No, it's only been six weeks. Does this email really need to be replied to this second? Or is it actually a Saturday and the recipient won't see it for a few days anyway? Taking a moment to assess each situation has definitely played a part in keeping some of the panic at bay.

Something Carissa Broadbent mentioned really resonated with me: "Focusing on what's really high-impact rather than expecting myself to do all the things has helped a ton, but I think it's very overwhelming no matter which way you shake it. I'm a pretty intuitive person, so allowing my intuition to guide me piece-by-piece rather than forcing myself to write down a mega-list or mega-plan all in one go has helped me a lot."

———

As you can see from my launch case studies, they've changed over the years depending on what I've learned about myself and whether or not the juice is worth the squeeze for certain launch tasks. A great example of this is the events. I went from intense parties of 100+ people to a more intimate gathering of 30 at most, and then to nothing, because I just didn't want to expend energy like that for the time being. This has taken away a whole load of stress I didn't realise I was carrying with each launch.

Where possible, I try to put restrictions on myself when it comes to working around a launch schedule. Sometimes the urge to work until the late hours is there, just to try to get ahead (if there is such a thing). But as someone who sleeps poorly at the best of times, I know that if I work past 8:30pm, all that churning in my mind will be even harder to silence come bedtime. Knowing yourself is half the battle when it comes to managing the crash-and-burn of big career events like launching a series.

Lastly, I find that prioritising the next book and getting it done helps remove some of the emotional weight from the current launch. I try to celebrate the milestone of releasing another book into the world, but I also make sure that I know what I'm working on next. And that's a nice segue into...

How do you manage to continue writing while launching? Do you create at all while launching a series?

This was a question sent to me from one of the lovely author communities I'm in. I opted to give it its own little section because I think it's an important one to address. Again, it's about knowing yourself and managing your expectations.

When I released the books in *The Oremere Chronicles*, I didn't create in terms of my body of work during launch. I was too stressed, too busy creating content, both for social media and for the platforms I was being featured on. It wasn't until the buzz of the launch had died down that I'd open up the book I'd been working on and try to sink back into it.

Now, I do things a little differently. Throughout the year, between writing projects, I schedule what I call "marketing and admin weeks". These are weeks where I'm not writing, but I'm ticking off all the things I've been putting off while drafting, editing etc. This is where I'll create launch plans, marketing strategies, content for social media, newsletter content. I'll try to catch up on reading industry news, and perhaps do some more market research to make sure I'm staying up to date with the latest trends and platforms that are working for authors.

Weeks like this, alongside my pre-order strategy rather than "live" launches, mean that a lot of the actual launch work is done well in advance. I'm no longer scrambling to send people links to Amazon when they go live; I'm no longer waiting until the last minute to book things. For the last four launches I've done, I've treated these periods like regular work weeks. If drafting is on the list for that week, it's drafting I'll do. Because I'm publishing more frequently now, I have to stick to my schedule, and I'm quite disciplined at doing just that.

The only exception is launch day itself. The day the book goes live is distracting as all hell, no matter how disciplined I am. Notifications are going nuts; even though I know I shouldn't, I obsessively check rankings and sales; and I want to be sure to reply to as many comments and posts about the book as possible to a) show my appreciation for my readers' support, and b) feed whatever social media algorithm is going on in the background. While I still try to get things done, I've usually created my to do list for that week with the distractions of launching in mind. Again, it's all about managing your own expectations. I don't expect to write 20,000 words during a launch week, so when that inevitably doesn't happen, I'm not beating myself up about it too much.

Post-launch blues

I've been talking about "post-launch blues" for years now, thinking there was something wrong with me when that inevitable high of launch wore off and I realised I had to do it all again… Turns out, I'm not the only one who feels this way. Of the authors I talked to, both in the research for this book and in general life, there's a real mix of us who experience the emotional crash after a launch.

For me, it's similar to Christmas (or any sort of holiday, really). You've waited and waited for the day to come, there's been all this anticipation and build-up to the event, and then it's over. And now there's another 365 days until the next one.

In Jenna Moreci's YouTube video "10 Things No One Tells You About Releasing a Book", Jenna talks about post-release burnout and how it can manifest in different ways: imposter syndrome, feeling lost and exhausted... Check, check, check. Yep, I've experienced all of these, and so have a lot of authors I've talked to. Again, this is where chatting with your author friends saves the day.

Marking the milestone

So often during launch weeks I'm asked what I'm doing to celebrate the release. The truth is, by this point I'm exhausted, and the more books I publish the more anticlimactic the launches seem to become. More often than not, they're just a regular working day for me.

I'm not the only one. Meg Jolly shared her experience with me: "On launch day, I'm usually knee deep on a new writing deadline, and stopping to think about launching pulled me in too many different directions and was frankly, stressful. I didn't celebrate at all, and it really was just another day at the office – which is a pretty miserable way to look at the mammoth achievement of publishing a book! After publishing so many – I think I'm at over 50 now over my career to date – it had lost its shine and become rather mundane. So, I vowed to change that."

While I'm nowhere near Meg's backlist of 50 books, I've started to feel the same, and so while I no longer do big launch events, I find it's still important to mark the occasion in some way to bookend the process, and to celebrate all the hard work I've done before moving on to the next thing. Usually, this is opening a nice bottle of wine with my partner, one we might have put aside especially for the occasion. Meg tells me that she tries to celebrate every launch as well: "I might buy myself a little treat, like a new crown when I publish a fantasy book/series, or a nice lunch or sweet treat that day, or [take] a walk in my favourite place – something that makes that day feel extra good for me, and pulls me out of that routine to mark it positively."

We're on the same page there. Even something small can make the whole thing seem a little less anticlimactic. I find it harder to keep the post-launch blues at bay if I haven't done anything to mark the milestone. As someone who's very future-driven, I'm often already onto the next thing without pausing to acknowledge that I've just achieved another goal. However you celebrate, big or small, I truly believe it's important to mark the milestone.

Taking a break

Whether it's a few hours, a few days or a proper holiday, I find that I always need some sort of buffer between the craziness of a launch and burying myself back into production mode. It's a lesson I have to teach myself time and time again.

Just take a look at this journal entry as an example: "Decided to take four days off after *DoM*'s release. It's a mistake I make every year – not taking time to rest after the chaos and stress of a launch, so here's to finally learning my lesson… I need it. My body is actually in physical discomfort after such long hours and sleeplessness over the past few weeks." (Author Diaries, April 15th, 2020)

Getting help

This book got bigger than I intended as I wrote it because I kept thinking of all the little things I wanted to share. While writing, I also went through the process of realising that my business was getting a little too big for me to handle by myself, particularly when it came to launches.

I decided that in order to focus on the things that only I could do (write the books, namely), I had to outsource some of the admin and marketing tasks to free up time and brain space. I'm certainly not saying that you need to hire help, or that you need to do everything I've listed within these pages; what I'm saying is that if hiring help is a feasible option, you have permission to do that. You don't have to do every task yourself.

Here are some of the things I outsource during launch periods to give myself a little more energy and brain space:

- Street team management
- ARC recruitment
- Outreach marketing research
- Newsletter swap research
- Newsletter formatting

If you're thinking about outsourcing, consider the things you like to do vs. the things you don't. Can you outsource some of the things you don't enjoy doing? I have an author friend who hates writing her social media captions, so she outsources this. Another has her assistant book all her paid newsletter promotion, and another has their VA schedule their social media.

Finding the right person can be tricky, as can training them, but after the initial teething problems, getting help can make a huge difference to that level of exhaustion during launch time.

When things go wrong...

The longer I've been doing this and the more books I've published, the more I realise how something goes wrong every single time. What I didn't realise when I launched my first series was just how common these bumps in the road are, and how they're not always the end of the world.

Chris Fox says it perfectly in *Launch to Market: Easy Marketing For Authors*: "Almost every launch has an issue. All we have to do is fix it, and move on. It can be tempting to obsess on it, but once you've done what you can to solve the problem try to let it go. We won't even remember it in a few months."

During the lead-up to the launch of *Heart of Mist*, I kept finding formatting errors in the paperback, not to mention that the local printer made my proof copy covers gloss, not matte, which took a bunch of back-and-forth to sort out. It doesn't sound like much, but for a first-time author trying to make sure everything was "perfect", I found it incredibly stressful. I've had issues of varying degrees with every launch:

- Ingram changed their printing times without warning
- Amazon temporarily terminated my account (on launch day, no less)
- Books didn't arrive to influencers on time
- Hardcovers for influencers arrived without the dust jacket
- Teething problems with new editors and cover designers put me in the midst of unplanned, intense deadlines
- Ingram allowed pre-orders when the book wasn't ready yet
- A proof copy took over six weeks to arrive, eating into my production schedule

I don't tell you this to scare you, but rather so you know that these things happen to everyone, and that hiccups during launch are more common than you might realise. We don't talk about them as much as we should for fear of looking like failures, but these things are happening more often than authors care to admit. A lot of this career is problem-solving, both with your writing itself and the marketing/publishing side of things, and launches are no exception.

With the problems I mentioned above, the solutions were often a combination of several things, like:

- Seeking help/advice from author friends or the Alliance of Independent Authors (in the case of account termination and teething problems)
- Communicating openly with my readers (in the case of delays and errors out of my control)
- Questioning whether or not the issue was as disastrous as I initially thought
- Shifting my mindset (in the case of most issues) to acknowledging that I was doing my best and that I needed to be kind to myself

The best we can do is to take a breath, try to solve the problem, seek help where needed and move on. As authors in an ever-changing industry, it's also important that we stay adaptable and are able to pivot and/or change course where needed.

TWENTY-THREE

Common Mistakes and Lessons Learned

"You learn so much more when you make mistakes, when things don't go the way you want them to... I don't have to get everything right every single time. I don't have to become a millionaire this month. We can slow down and stay the course and stick to the plan. And that's usually the better option."
—Steffanie Holmes

SO MUCH OF what I've learned about launching series over the years has been through trial and error. Even if you complete courses and read numerous books on indie publishing, sometimes there are factors that are unpredictable or unique to you and your situation.

I like to think that throughout this book I've been quite candid about where I've gone wrong and how I fixed those mistakes, or overcame them. Undoubtedly, though, there are things that didn't quite fit neatly into the previous chapters, so I want to share some additional experiences with you now in the hopes that you can avoid making the same mistakes. I'll also cover a few common mistakes I see newer authors make as they release their first series, and draw upon some of the conversations I had with other authors during the research phase for this book, sharing their experiences as well.

So here we go… Let's talk about mistakes and lessons learned.

Not managing expectations

This has been a massive lesson for me over the course of my career so far. Between publishing my first and second series, I had very little idea of how to compare the success of each of them beyond sales figures. I expected sales to just get bigger and bigger, and didn't take into consideration the myriad of other factors at play. I didn't set specific goals; I just hoped for the best, and "the best" was an unrealistic expectation, to say the least.

This led to some pretty crushing disappointment, despite the fact that the second series was still well received and sold well. My expectations had just been completely out of whack. When it came to launching my third series, I was a lot more cautious with my expectations. As I discussed earlier, I set a range of goals and mapped out what I felt would be a good trajectory for a new series in a new subgenre.

Rachel McLean talked about managing her expectations in our Q&A and shared the following: "I base my expectations on pre-orders but I do have a goal of getting a higher ranking for each launch. It doesn't always work as it depends so much on what books come out that week and the time of year."

Not tracking data

Not tracking my word counts and how long it takes me to complete various stages of book production was definitely one of my earlier mistakes. Without this information, it's difficult to predict how many books you'll be able to produce and therefore publish, and without *that* information, I struggled to come up with a solid launch strategy for the series.

Nowadays, I do my utmost to track everything, which makes coming up with launch plans and strategies far easier for me.

Discounting too soon

This is not something I've done myself, but something I've seen newer authors do from time to time: discounting their book (usually the first in a series) too close to release (which was at full price) and upsetting their most loyal readers.

What is "too soon"? It depends on how many books you're releasing and at what rate, but personally, I don't discount a book until at least six months after its full-price launch. The only exception for this would be if I managed to get a BookBub Featured Deal and I wanted to snatch up that opportunity, as they don't come around that often.

Rushing releases

In the indie publishing world, there is always a lingering pressure to produce more and publish faster, and sometimes we can get caught up in this. But when we rush our releases, that's when mistakes happen – avoidable mistakes. Perhaps you click the wrong cover finish when setting up your print book; perhaps you accidentally delete a whole chapter while formatting. Maybe you use a keyword that's flagged as a content breach on Amazon (that one actually happened to me).

The thing is, putting pressure on yourself to be faster can work in your favour, so long as it doesn't overwhelm you to the point where you're no longer paying attention to the finer details.

Stopping promotion too soon

We've already talked about the burnout that can sometimes accompany book launches, but in a similar vein, many authors take their foot off the promotional accelerator too soon, for fear of burning out their readers with their posts. I verbalised this worry to a very successful author a while back and her response was to tell me that you can never talk about your books too much. She said you can talk about an upcoming release until you're blue in the face and you'll still get messages that say, "I didn't know you had a new book out".

Since that conversation, I've stopped worrying about promoting "too much". Months after my most recent release, I'm still pushing that book one nearly as hard as I did in the lead-up to launch: sharing snippets, reviews and pretty pictures... And it's still finding new readers.

Not having a series launch strategy

When I released *Heart of Mist*, I certainly had a launch strategy for that particular book, but beyond "releasing book two next year", I didn't have a strategy for the overall series launch. This was partly due to the lack of data I had about my production rate, but it was also that I didn't know how much easier life would be if I had a plan in place for the whole series.

Armed with more information, I've been able to determine how many releases I can manage a year, which in turn informs my promotional efforts and how I stagger my launch marketing throughout the year. It determines when I do things like title and cover reveals, as well as street team sign-ups and ARC campaigns. It also helps me decide when to focus on the actual writing and when I can afford to take time to focus on admin/marketing, or – *shock horror* – take time off.

Not reviewing your business finances

We covered money briefly earlier, but my instinct in this area has always been to have a rough idea of things and not look too closely. That's born of fear – fear that I'll discover I'm not doing as well as I thought, fear that I'll find out I've made a huge mistake somewhere, and fear that I won't understand what I find. However, this is a business, and business is about money. Over the years (and after firing two accountants), I've gotten better at managing my own finances. I look even when I don't want to look, even when I know it's going to upset me.

Each month, I do my own profit and loss statement where I examine the income and expenses for my business (and yes, I absolutely have a separate bank account for this). I review subscription services, advertising costs, freelancer expenses and any fees I've been charged. I make sure everything is right (that I haven't been charged twice for anything, for example) and then I interrogate whether or not I need particular services for the next month or so, or whether or not commissioning that extra piece of art was a good investment.

This is an ongoing exercise – monthly, yearly and actually with each release as well: doubling down on the things that provide a good ROI and cutting out anything that is no longer needed or was a poor investment.

As I've mentioned, I'm certainly not a financial expert by any stretch of the imagination, but I have learned that in order to run a lean and profitable business, you need to review your finances regularly.

Not formatting back matter for optimal read-through

This is one I was certainly guilty of in the earlier years of my career. I packed my back matter full of too much info and fluff, and too many options for readers. As we covered in the chapter on back matter, now I streamline this as much as possible and make it very simple for the reader to click "Buy now" or "Pre-order" on the next book in the series.

———

No launch is ever going to be perfect. The important thing is that you learn from your mistakes (or the mistakes of others), and adjust your course and your plan accordingly for next time.

TWENTY-FOUR

FAQs

"I give myself a lot more grace for the time of life I'm in now."
—Krystal Shannan

IN THE RESEARCH for this book, I approached several author communities and asked them about their concerns and struggles when it came to launching a successful series. I've tried to answer everything in detail throughout the main content, but there were a few questions that came up time and time again that I would like to address here as well. So, let's get stuck into the FAQs of launching a successful series…

Q: How is launching a series different from launching a standalone novel? What would you do differently?

A: I think a lot of the launch strategies explored in this book can be used for both series and standalone titles, and that the choices are up to each individual author. However, I'd say the main difference is how you market and advertise the next book in the series. Launching a standalone arguably means having to convince readers to invest in new characters etc. all over again, whereas the next book in a series already has a warmed-up audience who wants to know what happens next.

Strategies between series and standalones can also vary in terms of the promotional push of the first book. Particularly if you're writing a dynamic or sequential series, you're always going to be driving traffic and readers to the first book, even when you're launching the tenth.

In a similar vein, your marketing for things like ARC and influencer campaigns will vary for a series, as the person you're targeting will need to have read the previous books.

Q: How do you determine the read-through rate or sell-through rate of a series?

A: "Read-through rate" is a term usually associated with determining the page reads of subsequent books in a series enrolled in Kindle Unlimited, while "sell-through rate" refers to the paid sales of subsequent books in a series. I've seen the two terms used interchangeably, but it's worth understanding the distinction. They're slightly different calculations, and depending on who's asking, the answers can hold more weight with different people in the industry.

In order to calculate read-through and/or sell-through, you need a number of books out in your series and a period of time to gather that data, so this may or may not be relevant to you just yet.

Like many authors, I'm no maths whiz, and frankly, the idea of numbers makes me cringe… But numbers are important for making decisions about your series and determining your success. Whenever I need a reminder of how to calculate these things, my favourite resource is Malorie Cooper's article for Kindlepreneur, "How to Calculate Series Read-Through (And Why It's Important to Know)", which I strongly recommend checking out. Thankfully, there are several calculators available for free online to get you started with this task, including the one at the bottom of Malorie's blog post, which I'll link to in my References section.

For the purpose of this section, let's take a quick look at calculations together…

Read-through rate

This is a little fiddly, as you'll need to find out the KENPC (Kindle Edition Normalised Page Count) for each book in your series (you can find this in your KDP dashboard). When you have this information for each book, you'll need to divide your KU pages read by this figure to get your total books read for the period of time you're assessing.

For example, if book one of a series had 2,602,130

"KU page reads" and its KENPC was 553, the calculation would be 2,602,130 ÷ 553, with the total reads amounting to 4,705.5. That's book one. Then you need to do the same calculation for the subsequent books in your series. Once you have the total reads for all the books in your series, you can determine the read-through rate with the following calculation: *book two total reads ÷ book one total reads*, and so forth.

For example: book two at 3,061.7 total reads ÷ book one at 4,705.5 total reads gives us a read-through rate of 0.65, meaning 65%.

For a series of three books, it might look something like this: book three at 2,298 total reads ÷ book one at 4,705.5 total reads gives us a read-through rate of 49%.

One thing I've been debating here is whether to include what a 'good' read-through (and sell-through) rate looks like. Given the number of variables and individual goals it's hard to pinpoint what that is. What is more helpful is to say that whatever your spend on book 1, especially if you're using it as a loss leader, your read-through and sell-through needs to bring you enough income and profit to make you happy and help you hit your goal. I encourage you to see how you feel about your own, with all the various factors in mind, and find some fellow authors you trust who you can compare with.

Sell-through rate

Take the sales of the subsequent and/or final book in your series and divide that number by the sales of book one. For example, if an author sells 2,283 copies of book one in their series, and 836 copies of book four, that gives us: $836 \div 2{,}283 = 36.6\%$, meaning that of the people who bought book one, 36.6% went on to buy the final book in the series. It's worth doing this calculation between all the books in your series (book two $\div$ book one, book three $\div$ book two and so on), so you can see if/where readers start to drop off in the series. The longer the period of time you have for this calculation, the more accurate data you'll have, so three months of sales would provide a more accurate result than a calculation within one month of launching that latest book.

––––––

Of course, these aren't 100% bullet-proof methods. It's worth noting that for the first little while, your read-through figures may be skewed on account of people snatching up the first book for free or at a discount, but never actually reading it and therefore not continuing on with the series. The launching of boxed sets can also have an effect on the results of these calculations.

Once again, I want to stress that this definitely isn't my area of expertise. Check out Malorie's blog post or the numerous other resources online on the topic.

Q: What is the most minimal way to launch for someone who is just starting out as an author?

A: Hopefully you will have seen some strategies throughout this book that have resonated with you, but the intensity and the budget of your launches are completely up to you.

Ultimately, though, things will either cost you time or money, and you have to decide which of these you can part with. If you're aiming to create a backlist before investing in advertising and marketing, a soft launch might be the option for you, but only you can choose which strategies align with you, your brand and your goals. I wish there was a silver bullet option I could give you – but if that was the case, everyone would be doing this job.

Q: What are good things to do after the launch itself?

A: Again, it all depends on your genre, your goals and your budget, but for me, continuing the conversation about your book and series is always a good idea, be it via your newsletter, your social media or both. I've also found that announcing the next book and sharing your progress on it is a good way to continue the buzz and excitement of a launch. It shows your readers that you're as invested in the series as they are, that you plan to deliver a satisfying series arc, and that you're actively working towards that goal for them.

Experimenting with discounts/sales and pricing strategies is another way to breathe new life into the various launch phases. Many of the strategies throughout this book can be used not only in the lead-up to launch, but afterwards as well.

Q: A question about pricing... Rule of thumb seems to be [a] discount or free book one once you have at least three books in the series. Should book two be discounted as well, or full price?

A: This entirely depends on your broader pricing strategy. My books are all full price, and around the launch of a new book, I discount book one in the series to either free or $0.99 and schedule paid promotion for that title. Take a look at the other authors in your genre and examine what strategies are working for them, but remember that there's no "right" way to do this and you need to experiment with what works for you and your readership.

Q: How clear should the series release schedule be at the launch of the first instalment?

A: I've ummed and ahhed about this question over the years. When I first started, I announced that *The Oremere Chronicles* would be a trilogy and there would be one book a year. Now, with a bit more experience under my belt, I've realised how quickly things can change, both in our personal lives and within the industry. I also learned that I want to leave room for flexibility within a series – to respond to whether it's doing well or poorly, and to give myself the option to expand or condense where needed. Therefore, as of writing this book, I haven't announced how many titles will be in my current series (although I do have a rough idea myself). When I released the first book, the second was already up for pre-order, but beyond that next book, I haven't given more information.

The thing is, you do set a precedent when you release regularly, and readers will come to expect that. I've gone from one to three fiction titles a year, and my audience knows they can generally expect more than two books a year from me now.

However, the most important aspect of all of this is communication. Communicate with your readers about when they might expect the next instalment, communicate your goals, and keep that line of communication open. Plus, these updates about your work serve a dual purpose of generating content you can use in your newsletter and social media.

Q: Is rapid release the best practice? Or does it risk compromising quality?

A: I know we've already covered this and that I'll probably sound like a broken record at this point, but the only best practice that exists is the best practice *for you*. Some authors can happily write and publish a book a month and maintain their professional standard of quality. Some authors, like myself, cannot. I've come to understand this through refining my own processes over the years. I can't rapid release. Or, I'll rephrase that – publishing four books a year? That *is* rapid releasing *for me*. It's up to you to work out if you can rapid release, what that looks like for you and if you're happy with the quality.

Q: Should you release one reader magnet prior to each subsequent instalment of the series, or just before book one and pull people into the funnel that way?

A: Again, there's no right way to do this, but I'll tell you my experience... I've done this a few different ways. I released three magnets before a book one (*Heart of Mist*) and three in between each subsequent release. I released one before a book one (*A Lair of Bones*) and then one in between the following releases. I have also released one before a book one (*Blood & Steel*) and then none (as yet) in between subsequent books. All have worked well for me.

I have pivoted in that the "bonus content" I utilised after *Blood & Steel* was an alternate POV scene, which was far less work than writing a whole new short story or novella.

For me, with the increase in the number of books I'm producing and publishing, I don't have the energy or time to write entire self-contained stories/novellas to give away for free between each release. So as of right now, I'm sticking with a complete reader magnet before book one, and then some lower-effort bonus content throughout the release of the subsequent books in the series.

Q: What's different when launching a fiction series vs. a nonfiction series?

A: From personal experience, the style of content marketing is quite different. For my fiction, it's all about getting my book in the hands of influencers and lovers of that particular genre; it's about swapping with fellow authors and creating beautiful photos and TikToks of my books. For a nonfiction series, the content marketing is more about *answering a specific question*. For this book in particular, I try to answer the question: how does one launch a successful series? And the nonfiction series itself, *Books For Career Authors*, tries to answer the question of how to become a successful author as a legitimate career. These particular answers inform the style of launch marketing I do, which is largely based around content marketing in the form of podcasts and guest post articles.

For me, fiction and nonfiction series launches are also very different in that they have vastly different release schedules. My current aim is to publish one book a year in my nonfiction series, whereas in my fiction series I'd like to publish two to three. This informs a variety of factors – for instance, when I launched *How To Write A Successful Series*, I didn't set a pre-order for this subsequent book, because while I knew it would be out in 2023, my fiction titles were my main priority.

Q: How do you plan your communication to not overwhelm people with too many books in a small timeframe?

A: This is definitely something I consider when planning my newsletters and social media content. In my newsletter, I try to segment the upcoming releases into their own sections under appropriate subheadings. On social media, I always refer people to the link in my bio, which has information on my upcoming releases.

Another thing I've started doing in more recent times is

posting FAQs on my social media profiles. These FAQs can include:

- How many books in the series?
- What is your next release?
- What is the release schedule?
- What formats will the book be available in? (Particularly important when simultaneous releases of audio aren't always possible)
- Does this take place in the same universe as your other series?

I've seen other authors create FAQ posts like this, as well as infographic-type posts that showcase the series reading order.

Q: For promotion, are you focusing on book one or do you have ideas to use the following books to lure readers in?

A: This is a tricky question, because the longer you do this job, the more it becomes a matter of luring readers not just into one series, but multiple. I try to strike a balance between promoting the first book in my current series (content marketing, paid advertising, influencer marketing and price promotions), the upcoming book in the series (content marketing and influencer marketing), and my other completed series (content marketing, price promotions, paid advertising, boxed sets).

I write dynamic series for the most part, so a reader always needs to read book one in order to understand the rest of the series, which is why the balance of promoting that first book is so important. However, I do find that as I promote the subsequent books in the series and gain visibility there, readers will click on my profile and start with the first book if the following ones have caught their attention.

All the techniques I use to funnel people into my series are covered in the earlier sections of this book.

Q: How could you test your launch strategy while in the midst of it? And how would you iterate or pivot halfway through?

A: Generally, the only thing I'm testing during my launch period is paid advertising. I keep an eye on the cost of things and tweak accordingly. I also keep an eye on the budget for sending copies to influencers, as this can get expensive. Other than that, I leave my assessment and pivoting until after the launch, when I have all the data I need to determine whether or not the launch was a success.

Other authors might do this differently, but I don't see the point in changing things halfway through before I have the complete data for analysis.

Q: What are your winning strategies to make people read the next book in the series?

A: This is a combination of the ending of your actual book and the way you've written and formatted your back matter. I encourage you to read *How To Write A Successful Series* for in-depth advice on the former, but in short, it's utilising things like breadcrumbs, open loops and cliffhangers, while the latter is covered earlier in this book in the chapter on back matter.

Conclusion

This book has been simmering at the back of my mind for a few years now. Every time I have launched a fiction title in my series, I've thought long and hard about the highs and lows I wanted to share with people.

The main lesson I have learned across these launches is that no two are quite the same, and yet the more you publish, the more the way you feel about them changes. I truly believe that the game isn't won or lost on the back of one launch, or even the launch of one series. This is a long game, a marathon. Ultimately, it's about building an incredible backlist of linked series that a reader can work their way through.

As you've hopefully discovered within these pages, we can continually build on what we've done, for decades to come. Our careers don't hang on the launch of a single book. No hit launch or launch flop is going to be the end of the story for us. And as Steffanie Holmes so wisely said, "We get to earn from these books forever".

I was concerned about how I was going to condense so much information as well as strategies that were so unique to each individual author. There's a lot to unpack here, but it's my hope that I've offered you a myriad of options to choose from, to experiment with and to apply to your own launches, so that you might launch your own successful series in the way that suits you.

When I asked Krystal Shannan what strategies she uses to set herself up for series success in the long term, she laughed and told me, "Ten years of learning what I like to do", and that resonated with me deeply. At the time of writing this book, I'm not quite a decade into my career, but "doing what works for you" and "learning what you like to do" have been themes throughout these pages, and they're lessons I'm clinging to as I prepare for countless series launches in the future.

As I wrote in *How To Write A Successful Series*, "there's no limit to learning", and I don't plan on stopping anytime soon.

If you've made it to these final lines, like me, you're in it for the long game.

So, what are you waiting for? Let's get launching.

References & Resources

Interviews

Throughout this book I quoted the following successful series authors: Carissa Broadbent, Steffanie Holmes, Meg Jolly, Rachel McLean, Clare Sager and Krystal Shannan. These authors were kind enough to generously offer their time to answer my questions in the form of video interviews and written Q&As. Without the insights and experiences they shared, this would have been a very different book, and I'm forever grateful to them for their input. You can find out more about each of these wonderful authors below:

- Carissa Broadbent: https://carissabroadbentbooks.com/
- Steffanie Holmes: https://www.steffanieholmes.com/

- Meg Jolly (Meg Cowley): https:// megjolly.com/ & https://megcowley.com/
- Rachel McLean: https://rachelmclean.com/
- Clare Sager: https://claresager.com/
- Krystal Shannan: https://www. krystalshannan.com/

References

Cooper, Malorie. 2022. "How to Calculate Series Read-Through (And Why It's Important to Know)". Kindlepreneur. December 13, 2022. https:// kindlepreneur.com/calculate-series-read-through.

Corder, Honorée. 2023. *You Must Market Your Book: Increase Your Impact, Sell More Books, and Make More Money.* Honorée Enterprises Publishing, LLC.

Erik, Nicholas. 2020. *The Ultimate Guide to Book Marketing: The 80/20 System for Selling More Books.* Independently published.

Erik, Nicholas. 2022. "Two Launch & Promo Tricks." Marketing Newsletter.

Fox, Chris. 2017. *Launch to Market: Easy Marketing for Authors* (Write Faster, Write Smarter Book 4). Independently published.

Gaughran, David. 2023. "Best Book Promotion Sites in 2023." David Gaughran. March 23, 2023. https://

davidgaughran.com/best-promo-sites-books/.

Hill, Whitney. 2023. "Leveraging Back Matter Content." Writer's Digest. June 17, 2023. https://www.writersdigest.com/be-inspired/leveraging-back-matter-content

Sansevieri, Penny. 2022. *From Book to Bestseller: The Savvy Author's Guide to Book Promotion, Smart Branding, and Longterm Success*. Independently published.

Scheuerer, Helen. 2022. *How To Write A Successful Series*. Independently published.

Resources

Throughout this book I mentioned numerous tools, courses and concepts, and you can find them informally listed below.

- "10 Things No One Tells You About Releasing a Book" – Jenna Moreci via YouTube: https://www.youtube.com/watch?v=z2gc1_7NLXc
- "Rapid Release Marketing" – 20Books Vegas 2021, Day 1 – Elana Johnson via YouTube: https://www.youtube.com/watch?v=yEW3iDtd-HQ
- *Wish I'd Known Then* podcast with Sara Rosett and Jami Albright
- "Writing for Your Id" presentation via Romance Writers of America by Jennifer Lynn Barnes

- *7 Figure Fiction* by T. Taylor
- *Amazon Ads for Authors: Tips and Strategies to Sell Your Books* by D. M. Potter
- *Amazon Decoded: A Marketing Guide to the Kindle Store* (Let's Get Publishing Book 4) by David Gaughran
- Book Brush: https://bookbrush.com/
- *BookBub Ads Expert: A Marketing Guide to Author Discovery* (Let's Get Publishing Book 3) by David Gaughran
- BookFunnel: https://bookfunnel.com/
- BookVault: https://bookvault.app/
- Canva: https://www.canva.com/
- David Gaughran's Starting From Zero course (free): https://davidgaughran.com/startingfromzeroresources/
- *Dear Writer, Are You in Burnout?* by Becca Syme
- Discord: https://discord.com/
- Draft2Digital: https://www.draft2digital.com/
- *Help! My Facebook Ads Suck*: Second Edition (Help! I'm an Author 1) by Mal Cooper
- *Indie Inspiration for Self-Publishers* series by Elana Johnson
- K-lytics Reports: https://k-lytics.com/
- KingSumo giveaways: https://kingsumo.com/
- Mailchimp: https://mailchimp.com/
- MailerLite: https://www.mailerlite.com/
- Mark Dawson's SPF 101 course: https://learn.selfpublishingformula.com/p/101
- *Newsletter Ninja* by Tammi Lebreque

- Nicholas Erik's author marketing emails: https://nicholaserik.com/start
- Rafflecopter: https://www.rafflecopter.com/
- Robin Reads, Fussy Librarian, Ereader News Today (ENT), Bargain Booksy and Freebooksy (see David Gaughran's blog post in References section)
- *Romance Your Brand* by Zoe York
- *Romancing the Beat* by Gwen Hayes
- *Self-Publishing with Amazon Ads: The Author's Guide to Lower Costs, Higher Royalties, and Greater Peace of Mind* by Bryan Cohen
- "Selling Books Direct On Shopify With Morgana Best", *The Creative Penn Podcast*: https://www.thecreativepenn.com/2022/08/08/selling-books-direct-on-shopify-with-morgana-best/
- "Selling Books Direct With Shopify: The Minimum Viable Store", *The Creative Penn Podcast*: https://www.thecreativepenn.com/2022/08/12/selling-books-direct-with-shopify-minimum-viable-store/
- SPF short course "Improve Your Launches" (within the 101 course)
- *Stop Making Others Rich: How Authors Can Make Bank By Selling Direct* by Morgana S. Best
- Vellum: https://vellum.pub/
- WooCommerce plugin: https://wordpress.org/plugins/woocommerce/
- WordPress: https://wordpress.com/
- *Writing and Releasing Rapidly* by Elana Johnson

Bonuses

Sign-up to my mailing list to receive my Successful Series Launch bundle, which includes:

- Ultimate *How To Launch A Successful Series* checklist
- Influencer pitch template
- Initial ARC email template for expression of interest applicants
- Reviewer call-out template
- A list of launch-related social media content ideas

In addition to the Successful Series Launch bundle, you'll also receive regular writing and publishing advice. Sign up here: https://helenscheuerer.com/series-launch-bonus/

Acknowledgements

As with my first nonfiction offering, this book is not just a product of the lessons learned, but of the shared experiences of those authors I love and admire as well, so as always, thanks are in order.

First, to the incredible authors who so generously donated their time and energy to talk to me about their own launch strategies, I'm so grateful for your insights and words of wisdom. Thank you to Rachel McLean, Krystal Shannan, Steffanie Holmes, Carissa Broadbent, Clare Sager and Meg Jolly. In addition, thank you to all the other authors who filled out my research survey; special mentions to Candace Robinson, Elle Beaumont, Lou Wilham and S. L. Prater.

Next, thank you to Sacha Black, who, during discussions about my first nonfiction book, told me that the idea was actually three separate books, if not more. This is the second of those books, and I'm so glad I listened. We'd be in a world of pain if I'd tried to put these 60,000+ word books into one volume, so thank you.

Of course, a huge thank you to the incredible authors who gave me permission to quote their work: Nicholas Erik, David Gaughran and Penny C. Sansevieri.

As always, a huge thank you to Gary Ditcher, the most supportive partner an author could ask for.

Thank you to my author friends Katlyn Duncan and Jenna Moreci for their ongoing support and quarterly check-ins.

And last but never least, thank YOU, my readers. I hope this book provided you with inspiration and options for how you can launch your own successful series.

About the Author

Helen B. Scheuerer is the bestselling fantasy author of the series *The Oremere Chronicles*, *Curse of the Cyren Queen* and *The Legends of Thezmarr*. Her work has been highly praised for its strong, flawed female characters and its action-packed plots. She also publishes advice for authors with her nonfiction series, *Books For Career Authors*.

Helen's love of writing and books led her to pursue a creative writing degree and a Masters of Publishing. She has been a full-time author since 2018 and now lives amidst the mountains in New Zealand where she is constantly dreaming up new stories.

Made in United States
Troutdale, OR
01/16/2024

16967538R00169